Mindfulness at Work

THE FUTURE OF WORK

Mindfulness at Work

KATHIRASAN K

Marshall Cavendish
Business

© 2023 K. Kathirasan

Published in 2023 by Marshall Cavendish Business
An imprint of Marshall Cavendish International

Other Marshall Cavendish Offices:
Marshall Cavendish Corporation, 800 Westchester Ave, Suite N-641, Rye Brook,
NY 10573, USA • Marshall Cavendish International (Thailand) Co Ltd, 253 Asoke,
16th Floor, Sukhumvit 21 Road, Klongtoey Nua, Wattana, Bangkok 10110, Thailand
• Marshall Cavendish (Malaysia) Sdn Bhd, Times Subang, Lot 46, Subang Hi-Tech
Industrial Park, Batu Tiga, 40000 Shah Alam, Selangor Darul Ehsan, Malaysia

Marshall Cavendish is a registered trademark of Times Publishing Limited

National Library Board, Singapore Cataloguing in Publication Data
Name(s): Kathirasan, K.
Title: Mindfulness at work / Kathirasan K.
Other Title(s): Future of work.
Description: Singapore : Marshall Cavendish Business, 2023.
Identifier(s): ISBN 978-981-5113-78-5 (paperback)
Subject(s): LCSH: Leadership. | Career development. | Mindfulness (Psychology)
Classification: DDC 658.4092--dc23

Printed in Singapore

Contents

WELCOME TO THE FUTURE OF WORK

Today, as more people work remotely, as work-life boundaries become increasingly blurred, and as AI becomes a tremendous opportunity/threat in every industry, there is no question that we must re-examine the way we work. And we will need leaders with the wisdom to show the way.

This timely book guides readers on a journey of applying proven mindfulness techniques to negotiate the challenges of work in the digital age. Readers are empowered with skills and techniques to take charge of their job and their career, and in so doing, unlock the leader within themselves. By working and leading with mindfulness, we have the potential to not only thrive in our careers, but also make positive impact on our teams, our organisation, and our community at large.

The Future of Work is a game-changing collection of business books that explore the rapidly evolving landscape of work today. Within the next five years, many jobs will disappear, many will be created, but what is certain is that all will change. The titles in this new series, written by some of the most influential business leaders, thought leaders, practitioners and consultants in the industry, cover everything from business trends and technological innovations, to revolutions in work culture and the critical skills you'll need in order to stay ahead of the curve.

Introduction

This is a book on mindfulness. Yes, another one.

I am certain that this book you are holding is going to add to the growing list of mindfulness and mindfulness-based business books that have become very popular in recent years. Yet I have good reasons for writing this book, and I believe you have good reasons to read it, whether you are new to mindfulness, or have already explored some of the existing literature.

The world today is filled with uncertainty. The recent COVID-19 pandemic proved that to us without doubt. We are also on the cusp of a fourth industrial revolution, which is merging the physical, digital and biological worlds. Artificial intelligence continues to challenge how we evaluate our self-worth. Businesses, organisations and nation-states are struggling to keep up with the rapid changes taking place as we accelerate towards this unknown frontier.

In the world of work, as Generation Y (Millennials) and Generation Z enter the global workforce, under the charge of leaders belonging to older generations, we are witnessing a clash in working styles and beliefs about leadership. A shift in the way leaders lead is urgently needed.

This book addresses that need, by looking at Mindfulness-Informed Leadership as a wisdom that can permeate any leadership style, model or belief. At its core is the belief that we create value from within, rather than by forcing you to change your leadership style or beliefs. This is what I call the art of being a leader, not becoming one. This book is also valuable for self-leadership where you can learn to be effective in influencing others as well transforming your professional life to one that is meaningful, relational and satisfying.

A PERSONAL JOURNEY

I would like to begin by telling you a bit about myself. On the one hand, I hope that by sharing my journey, you will find points of connection that will help you better appreciate the value of what I have written. But more importantly, I want you to meet me as a person – as a fellow human being – rather than as a teacher, mentor, coach or leadership consultant.

I was born in Singapore and grew up in a small family in a two-bedroom apartment. In the early years, it was just my dad, my mom, my sister, and me. A little later, my parents decided to foster a distant relative of my dad's who had been orphaned as a very young child.

From an early age, my parents drilled into me the image of success as being either an engineer, a doctor or a lawyer. But what I wanted to be was a fighter pilot. I collected the military magazines that my father brought home from his work at the British Navy's base in Singapore. At age 12, I could tell you the maximum speed of the F-14 Tomcat, the F-15 Eagle and the famous Blackbird.

And then, when I was 13, my dad passed away suddenly. His death affected my family terribly. Those were the dark ages of my life.

Despite that, I managed to pass my high school exams and joined a tertiary institution, where I spent three years, obtaining a diploma in electrical engineering.

I then enlisted in National Service. After serving the mandatory 30 months, I started my first job – in the military. I never became the engineer, lawyer or doctor that my parents always wanted me to be.

Nine months into the job, however, I realised that I could not fit in. This was in 1996, and by then I had already encountered mindfulness philosophies (not the practices) two years prior. These had a tremendous effect on me, especially in my worldview and how I looked at people. The culture of the military is one in which hierarchy and authority are key to its effectiveness. I was a non-uniformed officer, equivalent in rank to a lieutenant, but I could not deal with the fact that respect and value were given to my decisions just because I was an officer. I felt that respect should be earned. My views have changed in some ways since, but at that time, I could not reconcile this apparent conflict. After working in the job for close to a year, I left.

I joined a relatively young IT company as a facilities manager. This was probably the most rewarding experience of my career, and I stayed on at the company for more than a decade. During this time, I watched the company grow from 700 staff to around 10,000. The external stakeholders I worked with included successful business owners, startups and small-medium enterprises from diverse industries. I got to work directly with the senior leaders of these companies.

The most important thing I learned in this role was the value of relationships. A healthy relationship is vital to project management and leadership, and a healthy relationship requires adaptation to whatever situations arise. While my preferred style of leadership was egalitarian, there were times I had to temporarily play the role of an authoritarian, when directive behaviour was called for.

Thereafter I made another switch, this time to join one of Singapore's largest telco companies, where I had the opportunity to lead projects that involved a larger pool of stakeholders. Again, I was working with senior leaders and this time working across borders with colleagues in different time zones. This was my last stint in the business world as an employee.

Having worked in three large organisations and having received a stable income all my life, I started to ask myself if there was some kind of meaning that I could create in my work. I decided to take a sabbatical. This was the beginning of a new stage for me, where my personal life and professional life started to become seamless, which in itself was a great challenge and lesson in mindfulness.

I went back to school to pursue an MBA. At the same time, I started a business with two partners that dealt with Culture Transformation, Organisational Development Consulting and Leadership Development. Soon after, I started the Centre for Mindfulness. I also started working with a global company based out of the USA, delivering performance solutions in the Asia Pacific and Europe-Middle East.

My current businesses and engagements allow me to travel around the world meeting people of different cultures, values, habits and behaviours. The first time I travelled out of Singapore as an adult was in my mid-twenties. My family could not afford holidays to faraway destinations when I was a kid. But since 1998, I have been travelling extensively in the Asia Pacific and the Western hemisphere, primarily for business. These travels give me countless opportunities to develop my cross-cultural competencies.

Alongside all this work, I have volunteered in a local organisation that serves the needs of the community economically, emotionally and spiritually. I started out as a youth volunteer and eventually became a board member, steering the organisation's vision and mission for about ten years, before retiring from it. At the time of my departure, the organisation had over 500 members and 100 volunteers. I learned much about the spirit of volunteerism, leadership, management, finances and more importantly the needs of people in different strata of society.

All this while, I have been continuously engaged in learning about mindfulness philosophies. In 1999, I met my teacher for the first time and with him I spent six years studying and learning through source texts in Sanskrit. I started teaching mindfulness as a volunteer at the age of 25 and have never stopped since.

THE ROLES WE PLAY

From my story, and your own experience, it is clear we all play multiple roles in our lives – some sequentially, some concurrently. The mindfulness journey begins with recognising the nature of these roles, and appreciating how they provide clarity in being a mindful leader.

Let me draw on my own life again to illustrate this point. The roles I have taken on have helped me in shaping my purpose.

The first role was being a lecturer at a local tertiary institution. In this role, I met budding young minds, usually in their late teens, who were on the cusp of embarking on their careers. I spent almost a year coaching them in preparation for working life. A little later, I taught them another important subject: contemporary world issues.

This class allowed me to delve deep into issues like climate change, politics, war, poverty, discrimination and many others that are relevant to the whole of humanity. While I had been aware of these problems prior to teaching the classes, I was not awakened to their urgency until I saw the statistics, research findings and commentaries. This was the first role that inspired me to write this book.

The second role was as a leadership trainer and consultant. I worked with primarily large organisations and MNCs in the area of people development. I had the opportunity to work with supervisors, managers and leaders. One thing that occurred to me was that all of them played similar roles yet they were different. In particular, I noticed that managers and supervisors in large organisations repeatedly felt that they had less control in shaping the organisation's culture. The leaders, on the other hand, expected change in the culture from the managers and supervisors. While the intention was the same, the perceptions were quite different. These were the very feelings I had experienced during my years of employment. Trust appeared to be generally low in such situations. Diverse research and survey findings repeatedly state the need for authenticity, trust building, ethical behaviour and a positive focus in leadership. My experiences and interaction with a diverse range of stakeholders repeatedly confirmed these needs.

The third role was working in "dead-end" jobs. During my school vacations I took on a series of jobs so that I could buy things I wanted without depending on my mother, who was widowed by then. My first job was as a production line worker in a factory that manufactured cans for aerated drinks. Later I worked in a moving services company. Then I worked in another factory, doing the night shift from 11 pm till 7 am. It was one of most routine and boring jobs I've ever done. I discovered with a shock that there were many co-workers who lived in Malaysia and crossed the border each day to come to work. They spent five hours commuting daily and a few of them worked 12-hour shifts for six days a week. During my tertiary education days, I worked as a technician during the weekends for a mobile disco company, where I set up and dismantled equipment for events.

These experiences allowed me to gain insights on the lives of people that we often see as the "others". We do not know what it's like to stand in their shoes, or work with them shoulder to shoulder. I was fortunate to have that experience, which helped shape my leadership and management skills.

The fourth role is that of a mindfulness teacher and practitioner, which really inspired me to look at leadership from a mindfulness perspective. I discovered mindfulness through spirituality, but as I practised it, I realised that it can be presented stripped of its religious and spiritual roots. It has gained greater credibility with scientific research, and offers benefits to anyone, regardless of their religious or philosophical subscription. I still continue to this day living my life with awareness, attention and acceptance to the best I can. I don't presume to have achieved mastery; rather, I consider myself always a work in progress.

One other role in my life has led me to this point, and that is as an inter-faith facilitator in a multi-cultural society. In Singapore, we experience the best that many cultures and religions have to offer, from different languages to racial identities to religious celebrations, etc. Growing up in Singapore allowed me to experience diversity, but it was mindfulness that allowed me to accept diversity. I do not believe that one culture is "better" than another. Instead I take the position that there is only a better response in every situation. Accept the current reality and respond mindfully – that is what brings out the best in us.

Giving you this background allows me to convey one important fact about myself, which is that I am ordinary. As I practised mindfulness, I did not become extraordinary; in fact it became clearer to me that I am indeed ordinary. Mindfulness and Mindfulness-Informed Leadership are for ordinary people who wish to be authentic and lead people in a way that brings the core of our being into our transactions with the world.

Bear in mind, finally, that while you take on all sorts of roles in life – sometimes two or more at the same time – the fact remains that you are a single person playing multiple roles. One thing connects all these roles, and that is the person that you are. That is your *being*. So be very clear of what you want first as a human being before looking at the demands of the various roles that you play.

HOW TO READ THIS BOOK

In this book, I would like to invite you to re-examine your assumptions about leadership through the lens of mindfulness.

In the first part of the book, we will start by going into what Mindfulness-Informed Leadership is and the need for it at this point in our history. We will look at six domains that have a bearing on mindfulness – namely Awareness, Attention, Acceptance, Action, Attitude and Wisdom – and how they interact with one another. This will form the foundation of your understanding of what makes a mindful leader.

The second part of book presents 56 mindfulness insights and eight mindfulness practices for leaders. This will take eight weeks to complete if you choose to read one insight a day. Each insight invites you to savour one particular facet of MIL. Like a mirror, your

mind naturally reflects on the ideas in front of it with curiosity and non-judgement.

You may find that the tone and approach of this book is quite different from other books on leadership, business or self-development. The book is structured and at the same time loose. This is deliberate. I am a man of science and a man of arts. I am a musician and I enjoy it when I write a tune and am not asked why. At the same time, I enjoy diving into the depths of logic and rationality. I have used this style to show you into the world of MIL.

At some points, you may find me a little contradictory or repetitive, but rest assured that the contradictions are necessary to counter the potential trap of polarisation. In many philosophical traditions, it is recognised that wisdom can only be discovered through paradox. The same belief underlies the appreciation and practice of mindfulness.

My purpose in this book is to present information to your awareness. And to let your mind transform on its own. This allows the *doing* to arise from your *being*, with a focus on the being of leadership. As you read this book, let go of your predictable thoughts, your ingrained behaviour, and your anxieties about *becoming* a leader. What you need to do is just read. Read with an acceptance of whatever the outcome may be. That is the best thing you can do for yourself.

Mindful Work, Mindful Leadership

WHAT IS MINDFULNESS?

Mindfulness has been defined variously since days of yore. For the purposes of this book, I am confining myself to modern definitions that have been used by secular practitioners. According to Jon Kabat-Zinn, the father of the modern secular mindfulness movement:

> *Mindfulness is the awareness that emerges through paying attention on purpose, in the present moment, and non-judgmentally, to the unfolding of experience moment by moment.*

In a review of various definitions of mindfulness, a group of researchers defined it as:

> *Broadly conceptualized... a kind of nonelaborative, nonjudgmental, present-centred awareness in which each thought, feeling, or sensation that arises in the attentional field is acknowledged and accepted as it is.*

Jeffery Martin, who researches personal well-being and transformation, defines it as:

A state of psychological freedom that occurs when attention remains quiet and limber, without attachment to any particular point of view.

Based on the three definitions above, one can deduce that mindfulness is both a practice and a trait. As a practice, mindfulness is essentially mental or brain training. This refers to the various types of practices such as awareness-of-breath meditation, body scan, sitting meditation, coping breathing space, mindful eating, walking meditation, etc.

Mindfulness as a trait refers to the effortless mastery of being anchored in a state of awareness constantly. This is when mindfulness becomes a habit, pervading our thoughts, emotions and behaviour, becoming our mental disposition. Also known as dispositional mindfulness or trait mindfulness, it is the outcome of sustained mindfulness practices. One leads to the other.

Mindfulness has become very popular today due to the experiments conducted by Jon Kabat-Zinn in the late 1970s at the University of Massachusetts. His work gave birth to Mindfulness-Based Stress Reduction (MBSR), the first evidence-based mindfulness programme. Further studies have confirmed that mindfulness can indeed bring very positive results such as reduced stress, emotional regulation, performance enhancement, increase in positive mental states, reduced depression, enhanced resilience, etc.

Since then, other variants of mindfulness interventions have emerged, such as Mindfulness-Based Cognitive Therapy (MBCT),

Mindful Weight loss, Mindful Education, Mindful Leadership, and Mindfulness-Based Strengths Practice (MBSP), among many others. What was originally an intervention to reduce stress and chronic pain has now led to a second generation of mindfulness movements where the focus is on enhancing personal performance and effectiveness.

I call this Mindfulness 2.0, a new version of mindfulness that leverages the strengths we already possess – rather than merely treating our problems – to enter into the world of mindfulness.

SECULAR VS RELIGIOUS MINDFULNESS

As you may know, mindfulness does have religious roots. It was born as a soteriological practice (i.e., concerned with salvation) in ancient South Asia, and was primarily practised by people of three religions, namely Hinduism, Buddhism and Jainism. It eventually spread across Asia, evolving along the way.

Contemplative practices are not unique to these three religions. Indeed they are found in all major religions of the world, in various forms. These can collectively be referred to as religious mindfulness. One distinguishing feature of religious mindfulness practices is that they are aimed at a religious goal built around religious beliefs.

The second school of mindfulness is called secular mindfulness, which is the focus of this book. In contrast to the religious school, secular mindfulness focuses on mental and physical health, and more importantly, well-being. This is the key differentiator.

A third school of mindfulness is "McMindfulness" – a much-commoditised version of mindfulness that has become popular by riding on the bandwagon of the secular mindfulness movement. I define McMindfulness as a phenomenon where teaching mindfulness is more important than practising it. The need to propagate mindfulness by teachers who themselves are yet to embody it gives birth to McMindfulness.

MINDFULNESS-INFORMED LEADERSHIP (MIL)

Mindfulness-Informed Leadership (MIL) leverages the practices and insights gained from the secular mindfulness movement to use it as an effective tool in leadership. Importantly,. MIL allows you to develop yourself as a leader and as a human being.

Today, in a rapidly changing world, we need a new type of leader. Especially now that we are entering the fourth industrial revolution, we need a different type of leadership wisdom to address unique needs. I view MIL as one of the effective ways to develop our competencies in this new and ever-changing world. In this book I will use the term "mindful leader" to refer to a practitioner of MIL.

One of the key premises on which MIL is built is that leadership is a role, not you. You have taken up the role of the leader voluntarily or involuntarily. Therefore, your identification with the role of the leader is artificial to your being and purely for the sake of meeting a functional need. I will expand on this as we go along.

Leadership, being a role, sometimes does come to an end. Sometimes it transforms into another role. I have worked with retired diplomats and academic professors who were unable to let go of their roles although their roles had officially ended. Like a marriage that ends by choice or naturally through the demise of a partner, leadership too has an expiry date. Recognising this fact is itself a great hallmark of wisdom.

I see leaders as a microcosm of a larger culture or sub-culture. People tend to follow and emulate the way their leaders think, speak and act. Hence, leadership has a significant impact on organisational culture. Mindfulness helps leaders to constantly be aware of the culture they envision and to align their thoughts, words and actions with that desired culture.

LEADERSHIP BELIEFS, IDEAS AND TRENDS

Leadership is not something new to humanity. Our earliest ideas about leadership go as far back as when we lived in tribes. There would usually be a tribal leader or village leader, who would usually be an elder or the most powerful member in the community. Over time, this structure slowly grew into a monarchy, where a king or queen had all powers. Their power was absolute. Control of the military and defences came under their command too.

As society evolved, another type of leader started to hold power in a state or country. These were the merchants, who paid taxes and ensured that society thrived. These were the business leaders.

As political systems changed around the world, politicians who were voted into office took over the role of the monarch. They either replaced the monarchical system or operated alongside it. This introduced yet another type of leadership.

All this while, there would also be religious founders, whose followers span political borders, and whose leadership is followed till today.

While leadership is nothing new, it is a subject that is increasingly being studied. There have been researchers attempting to correlate leadership with religion, politics, gender, race, political systems, height, weight, colour, age, etc. Everybody seems to be trying to answer the question: are leaders made or born?

The last two decades, in particular, have given birth to many new theories and models of leadership.

One result is that we are in the business of making leadership another business. And all of them tend to present a model of leadership that is defined by very senior leaders or sometimes charismatic ones. But leadership does not belong to the sphere of senior and middle management. It belongs to anyone who has a person following her or him.

When I worked with supervisors in an engineering environment, I found that modern ideas of leadership frequently failed. Most models assume a high degree of individual autonomy, but this may not be present in some cultures or settings. The Western world is known to be more individualist, while Eastern cultures tend to be more collectivist. Broad leadership prescriptions that neglect these variables simply do not work.

Another trend in leadership theories today is the attempt to paint a picture of leadership through the eyes of the followers. This approach often makes the leader play the role of support-giver, nurturer, or family member who cares for and loves his employees. The followers, on their part, tend to seek a leader based on what they like and dislike.

These ideas unfortunately mix up identities and blur the lines that we have drawn for the sake of social conventions. A good example would be the role of the secretary. Here is an apt quote from the TV series *Mad Men*: "He may act like he wants a secretary, but most of the time they're looking for something between a mother and a waitress." The things we do may overlap with other roles but that does not mean that the role gets transformed. We cannot be treating the secretary as our mother because she makes coffee in the morning every day.

Conventional leadership theories also make it seem as if leadership is only meant for the rare few who are charismatic and self-actualised. Some even allude to leaders or heroes like Achilles, Siegfried and Roland – all of them mythical! We perpetuate this fantasy by expecting leaders to become these heroes. This is a completely unrealistic expectation. You are bound to be disappointed and frustrated if you compare yourself against "superheroes". Such ideas about leadership lead to self-judgment when you fail and to a certain form of narcissism.

Leadership is not something fantastic. Rather it is about being effective in delivering what needs to be delivered and perhaps exceeding it. To accomplish this, you do not have to be self-actualised or charismatic or superhuman. You just have to be yourself, an ordinary human being paying attention to the essentials.

The other tendency in "great stories" about leadership and successes is that they are written in reverse. We love to create solutions and systems out of our life experiences by looking at them backwards, in retrospect. And then we prescribe the solutions forwards to the world.

This approach leads to the assumption that we can control results with certainty. It also assumes that the environment we operate in does not change over time. It is quite a feat to predict success with a formula. It is easier to come up with the "whys" and the "hows" after securing victory. Because you can then retrace the steps you took and write a wonderful account of it. As with so many things, this tendency is simply human – a point that has been echoed by Daniel Kahneman, the Nobel-winning psychologist, in his book *Thinking Fast and Slow*.

I wish we studied the predictability of success more than trying to reverse-engineer it. I have yet to meet a successful businessman who learnt it all from books. In fact, wisdom informs us that by the time you read a book about how to be successful and try to replicate every step of the author's prescription, the time and environment would have changed. This is the pitfall of trying to be a successful leader by reverse-engineering.

With technology changing at an ever-faster rate and the advent of so many "disruptive" innovations, this point has never been more relevant.

One aspect of life that has seen enormous changes is the blurring of the line between business and personal life. Through social media and pervasive high-speed internet, businesses have entered into the most private spaces of our life. They are redefining how we consume information, how we see ourselves, how we relate to the people around us. I do not view this as something unfortunate, but it is definitely changing the way we live.

MINDFULNESS AND BUSINESS

There has always been a perceived tension between mindfulness and business drive. Focusing on the present moment and reducing one's reactivity could be viewed as counterproductive to ambition.

Indeed, I know some mindfulness practitioners who have developed a distaste for profit and for being driven. There is a tendency for such people to focus on promoting the virtues of positivity, happiness and well-being while shying away from addressing questions of "success" and business drive. This perception creates an opposition between the two worlds.

This is not something new. The ancient practitioners of mindfulness were monks, renunciates, anchorites and itinerant ascetics. I call people with such tendencies "contemplatives". Edwin Bryant, a professor of Indology, has found that contemplative practitioners since 3000 years ago have always been challenging new technologies of exploitation, and shunning the life of securing and preserving wealth.

Mindfulness reconciles this apparent incompatibility by balancing one's drive with wholesome action. We often tend to view results in an "ends justify the means" fashion. Mindfulness regulates this view by allowing one to focus on well-being and the ethics behind the means. As a result, decision-making becomes clearer, more ethically informed, less reactive or impulsive, and hence more sound for business.

So what we need is not to convert people who focus on business growth and profitability into permanent navel-gazers. Rather, we need to meet them in their own space to inspire a certain wholesomeness in the way they view the world.

One of the strengths of MIL is its ability to bring self and organisational goals into balance. There should therefore be no fear that MIL will displace the profitability of a business, as a mindful leader's intention is very clear: to create sustainable results. This balance can be likened to the balance between the rational and emotional sides of the brain.

For this to happen, we need to recognise ourselves for what we are. That's what is going to help us be an effective, mindful leader. Each one of us is unique and we should never strive to be the same. We may seek the same things – happiness, enjoyment, autonomy, security – but we seek them differently. And that is what makes the world beautiful. Mindfulness makes this vision of seeing unity in diversity possible. MIL paves way to such a realisation.

THE DARK SIDE

More than ever, now is the time for a leadership based on mindfulness. It is not that the world was perfect in the past, but the problems that humanity suffers from today stand to be ameliorated as never before through the application of mindfulness. In particular, we are experiencing unprecedented disruption and fragmentation in our lives, our societies and the environment.

In the following pages, I want to look at some of these problems we are facing, and explore how a mindful leader can respond to them in a manner that leads us towards what I call wholesomeness.

Stress

Technological progress, instead of reducing stress by making life easier, has increased stress by making us dependent on technology.

With constant internet connectivity and social media access, we have become addicted to our digital devices.

This "digital stress" affects people of all ages, but the younger generation appears to suffer the worst. In research done by the American Psychological Association in 2015, it was found that Millennials and Generation X in the US were the most stressed demographic group.

In the workplace, both leaders and followers experience high stress. Leaders or managers with limited control, especially, have been found to be under more stress. A leader's behaviour also significantly influences the level of stress experienced by his subordinates.

Stress affects different personality types in different ways. Type A leaders – driven, competitive and time-sensitive – appear to experience more stress than Type B leaders, who are typically calm, stable and reflective. This does not mean, though, that a Type A leader should try and become a Type B, or that Type B leaders are never stressed.

Stress has always been something that mindfulness addresses. The first wave of secular mindfulness teachings was explicitly directed at reducing stress – the MBSR (Mindfulness-Based Stress Reduction) programme developed by Jon Kabat-Zinn was instrumental in popularising mindfulness.

My interest, however, is in helping you *prevent* stress instead of mitigating it. There is an additional value in stepping into the world of mindfulness not from a debilitated state but from a state of positive health and performance. It is from this state that we can take the next step in creating positive change within and without.

Youths at Risk

Incidents of youths engaging in violence, as well as being the victims of violence, have been on the rise around the world. The World Health Organisation (WHO) reported in 2016 that each year 200,000 homicides occur among youths. The victims and perpetrators are mostly males. Also, about 40% of youths are exposed to bullying.

One recommendation given by WHO is to develop life-skills programmes for youths, to help them in anger management and to empower them with social skills to resolve the problems they encounter without violence. A second recommendation is to use therapeutic approaches for these youths-at-risk. In either case, we need leaders around the world who can engage such youths mindfully.

Mental Health

The increase in mental health issues at work is quite alarming. Anxiety, poor work-life balance and job stress are common issues at work. All of these reduce productivity, adversely impact relationships at work, and potentially lead to long-term mental health problems. The truth is that even a job you love can cause stress due to overworking and prolonged hours.

Outside of work, one group that is especially vulnerable to mental health issues is the elderly. Some of the biggest debilities of old age have been found to be depression, anxiety disorders and even self-harm. Preliminary research suggests that mindfulness practices have a positive impact on psychological well-being in the aged, increasing mental flexibility and cognitive performance.

Income Gap

Another global phenomenon is the growing income gap. According to one report, 8.6% of the world owns 85.6% of the global wealth.

Richard Wilkinson, co-author of *The Spirit Level*, has found that income inequality has a direct co-relation with health problems, mental illness, drug abuse, imprisonment and violence. Countries with narrower income gaps were found to have fewer problems in these areas as well as being more socially connected.

One of the key points for reflection among leaders could be how large salary disparities in organisations could create similar problems.

Climate Change

Climate change is another huge issue that we need to grapple with. Global warming is disrupting weather patterns, raising sea levels and causing extreme weather conditions. There is an urgent need to review how we consume, and to remind ourselves that the demand for consumption creates an increase in carbon emissions.

I do not think that the responsibility for reducing carbon emissions should be left to world leaders, scientists and lobbies. All leaders should shoulder this responsibility by being mindful of how the collective habits of our organisations contribute to this problem.

Population Increase

The world's population has grown rapidly in the last two hundred years. Within that timeframe, we have increased in number from 1 billion to 7 billion. This is a great sign in that it shows mortality rates have been tremendously reduced by advances in technology and better medical facilities.

We are expecting another 3 billion on this planet within the next 30 years, which will bring the total to 10 billion. Some scientists are considering this the biggest problem facing humanity, even bigger than climate change issues. With rapid population growth, food supply will be unable to meet consumption demand. Energy use will shoot up, and due to this, fossil fuels will deplete faster, more people will migrate, and culture clashes will inevitably occur.

Political Conflicts and Sovereignty

Would you believe that only 11 countries in the world have been found to be conflict-free? It is not only Iraq, Sudan, Ukraine, North Korea, Russia and Nigeria that are facing intense conflicts within and without. There are also internal conflicts that are political, communal, ethnic and economic in nature.

It is not always an issue of sovereignty. There is also a new form of conflict – tribalism – where people of the same ethnicity, religion and political identity band together. This is serious challenge because it creates sub-cultures, thus impeding social integration.

I was once on a train from Singapore to Kuala Lumpur and met four tourists from Europe who were taking a long holiday in Southeast Asia. They had spent only one night in Singapore, which surprised me, as Singapore is perhaps the most developed city in the region. They said that in the time they spent in Singapore, they found that the people largely only mixed with those of the same ethnicity. This came as a shock to me as I had taken this reality for granted and it took someone from the outside to point it out to me. This is modern tribalism. It could be right in your backyard but you may not notice it until something very disruptive happens in your social fabric.

Spending Priorities

In 2016, $19.7 billion was spent on Valentine's Day in the United States. In 2016, the world spent about $1.69 trillion dollars on military expenditure. In 2015, we spent $100 billion on chocolates. On the other hand, it is estimated that $340 billion per year is needed to provide up to high school education for underprivileged children and youths. And $150 billion is needed for clean water and sanitation. The facts are so glaring that austerity is not what is needed to solve the world's major issues. What we need is prioritisation based on wisdom and wholesomeness.

Having briefly examined the dark side of the current world, one thing that you would have noticed is that all the issues are interconnected. They are all part of the bigger picture. The purpose of MIL, then, is to be aware of these needs of the world, regardless of whether we can do anything about them directly. Because our intention can make a great difference to our action.

THE BRIGHT SIDE

Not all is gloom and doom, however. Looking at the direction that research and businesses have taken in the last few decades, I see a desire for positive change among scientists, world leaders, business leaders, religious leaders and the common man, including the person who is reading this book (yes, I am talking about you).

So it is also important that we recognise the positive changes that have been taking place around us. These set the impetus for recognising wholeness and acting with wholesomeness.

Neuroscience

The phenomenon of neuroplasticity is perhaps one of the greatest discoveries in neuroscience. Contrary to popular belief, our brain changes as we grow. People used to believe that it did not. Scientific studies in recent decades inform us that our thoughts and activities significantly transform the brain. New neural pathways are created whenever different parts of the brain are used.

Research surrounding mindfulness and neuroplasticity has uncovered astounding findings. Meditation practices have been found to increase the thickness of the cerebral cortex, which is responsible for attention, thinking, awareness, cognition and language. Mindfulness enhances these functions of the brain, especially the pre-frontal cortex, which is responsible for executive abilities.

Long-term meditators also have more grey matter, which is responsible for muscle control and sensory responses, resulting in better emotional regulation and response control. This assists in enhancing the ability to *respond* to situations rather than *reacting*. This would also explain how the brain's tendency to revert to "autopilot" mode gets attenuated through mindfulness practices.

It has also been found that mindfulness increases the grey matter of the hippocampus. The hippocampus is responsible for memory and knowledge. Mindfulness practitioners were found to have better learning and working memory capabilities.

The amygdala is a part of the brain responsible for the flight, fight and freeze reactions – i.e., reactive behaviour. It is very useful in emergency and safety situations as it allows you to rescue yourself and others very quickly. However, an overactive amygdala or an amygdala hijack, as it is called, keeps the amygdala on alert all the time. This leads to a reaction in every situation instead of a considered response. Research has found that mindfulness reduces the size of the amygdala.

The parietal lobe is responsible for one's sense of space and surroundings. It creates the notion of separation in space, including the feeling of being separate from other people. When meditating, parietal lobe activity slows down. This corroborates the feeling of non-separation – the feeling of oneness with the people and things around you – that meditators feel. The upshot of this is increased compassion and reduced violence. We take care not to hurt others as we feel they are not separate from ourselves.

Personality Traits

Personality traits refer to our thought patterns, emotions and behaviour. The "Big 5" personality trait theory, perhaps the most widely recognised theory in the industry, defines five traits that people possess in varying proportions:

- Openness to Experience – being open to new experiences and welcoming novelty; disliking routine

- Conscientiousness – being very organised and structured

- Extraversion – being talkative, energetic and sociable

- Agreeableness – being cooperative, accommodating and obliging

- Neuroticism – being sensitive, vulnerable and prone to unpleasant emotions

People who practise mindfulness have been shown to be more conscientious and less neurotic. This is a great advantage for leaders as it builds their objectivity and helps them to see the bigger picture and the interconnection between seemingly disparate ideas and objects. Reduced neuroticism can reduce stress and vulnerability to negative emotions.

Positive Psychology and Happiness Studies

The advent of Positive Psychology by Martin Seligman challenged the way we view our well-being and self-perception. While traditional psychology limited itself to the study of mental illnesses, positive psychology delves into the subjective states of happiness, optimism, flow, contentment, satisfaction, hope, well-being, inspiration and meaning. It focuses on what human beings need in order to flourish.

Initially, positive psychology tended to treat the "dark side" as the adversary of happiness and fulfilment. With Second Wave Positive Psychology (PP 2.0), the dark side is embraced as natural. This makes it much better aligned with the vision of wholeness taught in mindfulness traditions. Wholeness is a complete vision and experience of the self, accepting all experiences without judgment but choosing to be positive in our response to these experiences with discretion.

Happiness studies have also challenged our assumptions about the purpose of life and purpose in life. Happiness is defined and described in various ways: subjective well-being, psychological well-being, hedonia, eudaimonia. We will look at these in more detail later, but one thing is very clear: the study of happiness is not confined to philosophy and religion.

For leaders, it's helpful to note that happiness is a good indicator of performance. Happy employees have been found to be more competent, more welcoming of change, more innovative and to contribute more positively to organisational performance.

Organisational Well-being

The vision of MIL is where organisations are not insentient entities but rather organisms in which people thrive. Organisational well-being challenges the traditional measurement of performance solely by financial performance and introduces other much-neglected aspects. It behoves leaders to recognise the importance of happiness, values, burnout, psychological well-being, positive emotions, stress, work addiction, coaching and health in the members of their organisation and teams.

I like to define business value via the "triple bottom line" (TPL): People, Planet and Profit. This concept, introduced by John Elkington, looks towards the larger responsibility of businesses, which is to contribute to a greater good beyond profits, hence contributing to wholesomeness.

Connectedness

The rapid advancements in communications technology in recent decades have made the world much smaller. I remember writing letters on paper to my friend in Brunei when he was doing his military service there for more than a year. It took two weeks for the letter to reach him and another two weeks for me to receive his reply. In 1996 I purchased my first paid email service, and communication became instantaneous. Now, we can connect with people in other parts of the world via social media, video calls, etc. We are more connected to each other than ever before.

Cosmopolitanism

Along with these technological advancements and the increased efficiency in communication and movement, population migration has become easy and quick. Every seventh person you meet is a migrant. As of 2017, there are 257 million migrants across the globe. The more developed countries attract more migrants, contributing to a more cosmopolitan society and diverse workforce. Organisations have also become melting pots where people from diverse cultures meet, interact and work towards shared organisational goals.

We Are Good People

Experiments were conducted at Yale University to find out if human beings are inherently good or bad. The impetus for this experiment was to find out if what our history says about ourselves is true. Our history is strewn with battles, conflicts, bloodshed and deaths. Even the most benevolent ideals have caused violence, exploitation and subjugation. This begs an inquiry if humans are after all good.

One way to do this is by observing babies, as they are yet to be conditioned by upbringing and influence. Professors Paul Bloom and Karen Wynn of the Yale University did exactly that. They found that contrary to earlier beliefs that babies are amoral, babies are in fact naturally good. Babies were found to possess rudimentary feelings of justice, and reactions to good and bad.

The implication of this research is that human beings have the capacity to live life in a wholesome manner. This is where I believe mindfulness can make a huge effect via neuroplasticity. It helps us to be positive and wholesome by paying attention and being aware.

Fourth Industrial Revolution

We are now at the cusp of another industrial revolution, as Klaus Schwab predicts in his amazing book *The Fourth Industrial Revolution.* The first industrial revolution was due to the invention of the steam engine. The second was triggered by electricity and mass production. The third was the digital age. In the fourth industrial revolution, we are now witnessing the merging of the physical, biological and artificial intelligence.

While the revolution will enhance our functionalities exponentially, it will also result in immense challenges. These include *computers replacing jobs, purposelessness in life, the need for new leadership competencies, etc.* Our ideas about morality and ethics will be severely challenged as the power to play God comes within reach.

* * *

While there are definitely positive developments on many fronts, none of them alone is a cure for all our personal and societal ills. A solution of today can become a problem of tomorrow. We need to celebrate the great progress we have made but at the same time recognise that not all parts of the whole have made equitable progress in well-being. We need, therefore, to keep a clear focus on how we as leaders can take big and small steps towards positive change within ourselves, others and the world.

A MODEL FOR MIL

MIL is a response to the needs of the world today and in the future. As leaders, we can utilise MIL to create positive change because it allows us build an inside-out orientation instead of working outside-in. The challenges we are facing and about to face require a different type of intelligence from before, one that has to arise from within ourselves, while not neglecting what lies outside ourselves. That is what MIL aims to do for leaders who are expected to influence, respond and accomplish.

I present MIL via six domains: Awareness, Attention, Acceptance, Action, Attitude and Wisdom.

The first three domains form the core of all mindfulness practices. Awareness is the domain where a leader enhances his ability to be aware of himself, others and the environment. Attention is primarily the recognition of the fundamental nature of human beings and the world, which provides an anchor for leadership. Acceptance allows a leader to respond to whatever situation is thrown at him with a sense of accommodation, without any kind of judgment.

Action is the domain where leaders allow their doing to arise from their being, while Attitude is about the wholesome leadership attitudes that influence Action. The final domain, Wisdom, also influences action, by imbuing it with the understanding that leaders are not islands and our actions affect others and the world we live in.

Let us now look at each of these domains in more detail.

Awareness

The first aspect in the domain of mindfulness practices that forms the heart of MIL is an acute sense of awareness or self-awareness. Awareness to me is perhaps the most important trait of a mindful leader. I consider it to be almost a synonym for mindfulness. It is a trait that defines your very being.

WITNESSING CONSCIOUSNESS

In mindfulness, awareness can be thought of as one's core, which is being. This awareness can also be thought of as a witness or *witnessing consciousness*, sometimes also called metacognition. It is in this awareness that all cogitations and actions arise. In an interview, Jon Kabat-Zinn made the remarkable observation that when you are mindful, the sense of doing arises from this being. There is no separation between this being and the sense of doing.

I liken this awareness to a movie screen on which moving images are projected. Without a screen, the movie cannot be projected. Every aspect of the movie – characters, storyline, action – is taking place on the screen. Mindful leaders consider themselves as a blank screen on which all their mental and physical activities take place. This is one reason why mindful leaders have greater resilience and control – they are detached observers rather than involved actors.

Another illustration that I like to use to explain witnessing conscious-ness is a soccer game. The players take on a variety of positions, such as goalkeeper, defender, midfielder, striker. The soccer field supports the game by providing a substratum for it to take place; the field remains the same regardless of what position you play. Sometimes you win on that field and sometimes you lose, yet the field remains the same. Each position has a different role, but they all work together to get the ball into the net. The winning team celebrates and the losing one weeps with regret. Yet the field remains unchanged.

Similarly, a mindful leader looks at his being (witnessing con-sciousness or awareness) as the substratum on which he plays his leadership role. Sometimes he succeeds, sometimes he does not. Sometimes he is the manager, then he might become a follower. But his awareness remains unchanged.

Being a leader is only one of many roles you might play. You also play personal roles such as a sibling, parent, child, spouse, grandparent, etc. All of these roles depend on you for their existence. But what mindfulness shows us is that your awareness can be independent of these roles. Indeed, witnessing consciousness is a definitive trait of mindful leaders.

SELF-AWARENESS

A specific aspect of awareness is self-awareness. Self-awareness is the practice and trait of noticing our inner experiences non-judg-mentally. It is the ability to be aware of one's thoughts, feelings, emotions, intentions, motivations and actions.

We are basically a bunch of thoughts. All external experiences, as objective as they are, get translated into internal thought-forms. Pain is experienced as thought and so is pleasure. That is the reason why we can be "without" pain when we are in deep sleep – it is due to the absence of thoughts. The pain returns the moment our thoughts return in our waking state. Clearly, our thoughts impel our intentions, decisions and actions.

Our intentions are also prone to being influenced by our natural biases. We make different decisions for people we love, people we hate and people we are neutral to. This self-interest is instinctive. We need not judge it because it is how we are built. Instead, we need to accept it and keep noticing how these biases profoundly influence our decisions and thoughts.

Emotions are yet another thing that have the power to influence us. Emotions can be better understood by noticing two aspects: valence and arousal. Valence refers to the positive or negative feelings we experience from an emotion. Positive emotions such as joy, interest, calmness and curiosity make us feel comfortable. On the other hand, negative emotions such as sadness, sorrow, anger, fear and disgust make us feel uncomfortable. Arousal is the physiological reaction that emotions are capable of inducing. It is notable that negative emotions induce greater arousal than positive emotions. That is the reason why we tend to regret our decisions and actions when we act due to high arousal.

It is also worth noting that positive emotions tend to lead to more wholesome actions while negative emotions lead to unwholesome ones. This is why self-awareness is crucial for a leader. When an individual gets angry, he creates chaos in his home; when a leader gets angry, he creates chaos in his organisation.

That said, a mindful leader doesn't repudiate all emotion. A good illustration of this would be the emotions we experience while watching a movie. We laugh, cry, celebrate and get horrified by so many things in the movies we watch, but the emotions go away soon after. While we tend to avoid negative emotions like sadness and fear in real life, we willingly subject ourselves to tearjerkers and horror flicks. We do this because we are aware that our emotions are constrained by the length of the movie, unlike what we face in real life. A mindful leader with self-awareness exercises this mastery by letting the mind be human, by letting it be itself.

Finally, the thing about self-awareness is that it reminds us that we are disposed towards enhancing the well-being of ourselves, others and the world we live in. It constantly informs us that our minds are programmed to fulfil this need or want naturally. Even the most insentient animal wants to be free and to seek out its comforts. Plants grow towards sunlight without needing anyone's command or permission. Our minds, too, behave in a similar manner. Self-awareness constantly reminds us of the innate nature of our minds.

OTHER-AWARENESS

*One of the secrets of life is that all that is really worth
the doing is what we do for others.*
— Lewis Carroll

Self-awareness advances us towards other-awareness, which is the awareness of others who are within our sphere of life. It is of utmost importance that we recognise that everyone is *"just like me"* – with minds that are innately programmed with self-interest, influenced by emotions, and focused on well-being.

It is not a requirement that others are as self-aware as I am. At the same time, there will be people who are more self-aware than I am. But all of them are *just like me*. The suicide bomber who just killed a hundred people and the altruist who gave away everything he had to help his neighbour are *just like me*. We do not know what situations would drive us to act like the people we admire and detest. People who commit wholesome and unwholesome deeds are *just like me*. It is not necessary for others to be mindful for me to see them as fundamentally non-different from me. *Just like me* is a powerful insight gained from self-awareness.

For leaders, other-awareness is crucial to success. It helps us to influence others more effectively. Without other-awareness, leaders resort to coercion, nonchalance or withdrawal. Being aware of others' intentions, values, emotions and thoughts helps mindful leaders make more wholesome decisions, with clear recognition of what needs to be done.

THE UNKNOWN SELF

Here is a great tool that can help deepen our self-awareness as well as our other-awareness, especially for leaders. Most leaders, by virtue of their role, possess a certain degree of power. The danger is that this power can obscure our awareness of our behaviour, values and the impact we create.

The following model, known as the Johari Window, has four "windows". Each window refers to aspects of a person that are known or unknown to the person himself and to others.

The Open window is where a person's traits are known to both the person himself and to others. This is the best space for a leader

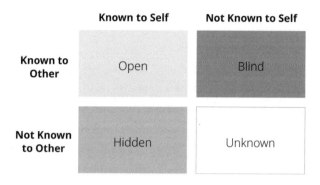

to be in because it creates trust and safety, and promotes greater awareness and transparency in his team or organisation.

The Blind window is where the leader's behaviour is known to others but not to himself. This is perhaps the biggest stumbling block for a leader. Typically, the only way to discover one's blind spots is by getting feedback from one's team members. However, getting feedback is quite a difficult thing for leaders as sometimes leaders do not want to hear the bad stuff or to look incompetent. But this is a window that needs to be opened. Not knowing one's blind spots hampers self-awareness.

The Hidden window is about stuff that you know about yourself but which is not known to others. This window remains closed due to not communicating effectively or not revealing enough about yourself. This creates a climate of ignorance in your organisation and can lead to people second-guessing your intentions. To open this window, a leader needs to open up more to his team members.

The Unknown window is the abyss. We do not know what is in there. Here is where psychometric assessments can identify possible psychological traits unknown to us and others. We may discover hidden strengths, weaknesses, behavioural patterns, etc., that we never knew we had. As with the Blind window, we should explore the Unknown non-judgmentally and with acceptance.

Mindfulness helps us open our Blind, Hidden and Unknown windows. Through self-awareness and witnessing consciousness, we can unearth aspects of our self not known to us. As we observe and notice our thoughts and breath, it is as if we are shining a brighter torch on our feelings and behaviours. And as a result, we also communicate with greater clarity, allowing others to understand us better.

AWARENESS IS WHOLE

You are already whole, already complete, just as you are
– and that is perfect – for now – in the warm embrace
of your own consciousness.
— Jon Kabat-Zinn

One of the deepest insights that mindfulness practices lead to is the discovery of awareness being whole. The definition of whole here refers to awareness being not of parts and identity-less. Awareness is like a blank canvas on which you paint your identities, roles, positions, thoughts, emotions, actions, etc. Awareness by its nature is devoid of all these roles but makes all of them possible by its presence, like the canvas.

I am aware of my intentions. I am aware of my thoughts. I am aware of my joy. I am aware of my anger. I am aware of my hunger. I am aware of being satisfied. I am aware of the chair. I am aware of my home. I am aware of my country. I am aware of the planet Earth.

All of these cognitions take place in our awareness. They arise in our awareness. Like a clear crystal that takes on the colour of an object that is proximate to it, our awareness takes on the colour of what we are aware of.

This awareness is therefore whole and complete without the need for any identity. It does not judge; it is always available in the present moment; it is just being; and it is what you are when you are naked without the clothes of identities, roles and presumptions. This awareness is the same in everyone for it is identity-less.

Attention

The second aspect of mindfulness practices is attention. Attention can refer to two related concepts: concentration practices; and the recognition and recollection of what is already known during mindfulness practices.

Concentration pretty much refers to paying attention and focusing on the present moment – essentially what is done in all mindfulness practices, especially the formal ones. Some people take it to mean that you must force the mind to fixate on a single object, but this is not the intention. Concentration practices in mindfulness primarily revolve around noticing with awareness and non-judgment. A simple concentration practice would be noticing your breath without changing the way you breathe in the present moment.

The other aspect of attention, which I will explore more here, is the ability to recognise the instinctive nature of human beings. Recognition, unlike awareness, has a character which acknowledges and confirms things as they are. This is something unique to mindfulness, where philosophy meets science. Recognition is the ability to acknowledge the facts of life and values that are common to all humanity. The recognition and recollection of universal ideas can take place as a meditation or even as a casual reflection.

DIVERSITY AND COMMONALITY

One of the first things for us to recognise is the inherent diversity of humans. At the same time that we all belong to the same species, we exhibit variation and difference. We live in different lands, speak different languages, eat different foods, appreciate different art, etc. Yet, all of us value the same fundamental universal values.

Leaders cannot afford to ignore or betray this diversity inherent in humanity. In fact, the fear of diversity, and the wish for uniformity, threaten the well-being of the world.

The mindful leader is attentive to the fact that all his team members seek happiness or well-being. In all civilisations, from the Chinese to the Indians to the Greeks, philosophers have tried to analyse happiness. The pursuit of happiness is innate to human beings. As leaders, we cannot ignore this.

That said, this is in no way a call for leaders to make their members happy at all cost. That is not the sole purpose of a mindful leader. A better way to go about this is to focus on well-being instead of happiness. Well-being includes happiness as well as physical well-being, emotional well-being, competencies and personal fulfilment. It is a more objective concept than happiness, which is more of a subjective psychological experience. As leaders, we should recognise well-being as a common good.

HABITS AND AUTOPILOT

Mindful leaders bring their attention to bear on the fact that habits can significantly affect the way they lead, as well as how others respond to their leadership.

ATTENTION

In a way, we are no more than a bunch of habits. Our habits are formed at a very young age and can become so deep-seated that we become unconscious of them. For example, I have a tendency to please people by accommodating them because as a child I was in the habit of avoiding conflict and uncomfortable situations. Habits can become "second nature", affecting how we operate, sometimes negatively. Hence the need to pay attention to them.

As we recognise the deep-seated "grooves" caused by our habits, we also pay greater attention to our TEA – Thoughts, Emotions and Actions. In my work, I have met leaders who were very suspicious of others, as well as leaders who were too trusting. We can all have such extreme polarities in us and it is good to pay attention to them without judgment. The motivations of our TEA can be seated in many things, such as our cultural beliefs and religious beliefs. We need to be very careful not to take the path of rational analysis to find the root cause of our TEA. What is needed is to notice them with curiosity during our mindfulness practices. This is adequate.

Habits and TEA influence another phenomenon in mindfulness: the autopilot. The autopilot is the instinctive (yet tameable) aspect of our brain. It is responsible for the reactive nature of the body-sense-mind complex, allowing us to do tasks without conscious thought. However, the danger is that it can also potentially prevent us from making decisions consciously and rationally.

If you happen to be someone in a position of considerable power, with many team members under your charge, there is a good chance that you may never recognise the autopilot in your leadership. That's because no team member is willing to challenge your authority, either out of fear, respect, or simply wanting to be agreeable. The more senior and powerful you are, the higher the chances that you won't recognise these things I am talking about.

When I am performing my role as a mindfulness teacher or leadership consultant, clients tend to believe what I say in the room on the basis of my position of authority. This is perhaps one of the most uncomfortable parts of my work because I do not want people to believe me because I said so. I want them to come to their own recognition of facts and truths about themselves or at least develop the curiosity to know more about themselves.

A charismatic leader tends to elicit admiration and emulation. People who idolise you for your leadership may start imitating you in terms of words, behaviour and actions. The pitfall here is that they cease thinking for themselves in a way that is true to their *own* beliefs and values. As a mindful leader, you need to do your best not to encourage such "idolatry".

Finally, I have found that mindfulness itself can be an autopilot reaction to a world that has gone wrong. Mindfulness is not a panacea for the world's ills. The world is far too complex for a single thing to fix it. We need to pay attention to the dangers of overdependence on pet theories, so as to avoid going down the road of dogma, bigotry and fanaticism.

TWO GOALS OF HAPPINESS

We talked earlier about how the pursuit of happiness is universal, hence the importance of giving it due attention and recognition during mindfulness practices. Let me go into this in more detail here.

The pursuit of happiness – in terms of how a person goes about it – can be understood as a continuum between two extreme dispositions. On one end is Hedonia, and on the other is Eudaimonia.

Hedonia is the experience of happiness via sensory experiences, while eudaimonia is the experience of happiness via meaning and purpose.

Everyone lies somewhere on this scale. Not recognising the existence of the two approaches can potentially create challenges for leaders. In particular, the biggest problem arises when a leader assumes that all types of people can be motivated and satisfied in the same way.

Eudaimonic people are primarily those who need to find meaning and purpose in their jobs and in life. Values are of central importance to their work, and they can sometimes be idealists. They are motivated by purposeful and meaningful goals. They may also expect others to be on a quest for meaning, the same way they are.

Hedonic people are more pragmatic. They enjoy material and sensory pleasures. Pride in their achievements and the esteem of other people are important elements of experiences for them. I have found that most people belong in this category.

Then there are those who pursue both eudaimonia and hedonia. For example, a person might want a meaningful job that pays very well. This is a mind wanting to find a purpose for its existence by finding something to do which will create hedonia. In my opinion, this tendency is ultimately hedonic as the end in mind still shows a hedonic inclination.

Between the two ends of the happiness scale, mindfulness tends to have a eudaimonic slant. Eudaimonia calls for objectivity in one's actions and responses, which should be wholesome for a given place, time and circumstance. As a mindful leader, you may have to take decisions that don't necessarily make you happy or make you look good (hedonia), but that you take anyway because it feels right to do the right thing. I call this discretionary action, i.e., allowing the doing to arise from your being.

Thus we do not look for a hedonic form of happiness in ourselves to be effective, yet we accept hedonia when it happens. In that way, MIL can be said to be thoroughly objective with a magnanimous allowance for subjectivity.

Liking what you do is a bonus but not a necessity in MIL. I am pretty sure that the many men and women who went out to protect their countries during crisis and war did not choose to do it because they liked it. This is the eudaimonia that I encourage among leaders as it is conducive to well-being and wholesomeness.

Acceptance

The third aspect of mindfulness practices is acceptance. Acceptance is the invitation of all experiences – including discomfort, distractions, rumination – with a sense of accommodation, without any kind of judgment.

MEASURING MINDFULNESS

Meditators tend to measure their practice based on two values – quantity and quality. It is common for someone to consider a 30-minute practice to be better than a 5-minute practice. Such measurements are primarily measuring the period of *doing* in meditation. However, nothing can really measure the *being* in meditation. Because being is all about being in the present moment. The present moment cannot be measured. In mindfulness, we are not looking for success in our meditations. The being of mindfulness practices does not depend on time. All we wish to do is to welcome everything that happens in our mind space. We welcome them like guests who come to our home uninvited.

The other common value of measurement is quality. I have had participants tell me that their meditation was filled with distractions and they were unable to stay focused. My usual response is to tell them to acknowledge the distractions and bring their mind back to where they want it to be. Even if you "fail" a thousand times, acknowledge it and continue to pay attention. So even measuring your quality of meditation is a judgment after all. The fact that "you are in meditation" is the truth of the present moment.

Yet, mindfulness practices do have a goal, in that we set out with a clear intention of wanting to be mindful, However, we then suspend that thought by just focusing on the practice. It is like having a set destination before starting a journey, but enjoying the journey along the way instead of being preoccupied with the end point. This is how we practise acceptance.

When we try to extend this practice of acceptance to our business and personal life, we usually find that it is a big challenge. One of the reasons is that as human beings we love to be in control and to control others. We are obsessed with specific favourable outcomes and we only want that and nothing else. The only way we know how to accomplish it is by controlling people and situations. Because we invest so much in controlling things, we feel miserable when they do not turn out as expected.

Perhaps the greatest challenge in practising acceptance is kicking the habit of equating our efforts with the outcomes. We expect to achieve a desired outcome based on our intelligence and the time and energy that we invest in it. When things do not go our way, we go into a negative spiral of emotions and reactions. This happens because of the strong sense of "doer-ship" we associate with the effort invested, and the assumption that we have control over the factors that influence the outcome.

ACCEPTANCE

A more mindful attitude is to "let go" of things that are not in our control. Accept that while we have better control of ourselves, the external influencers of outcomes are never within our control entirely.

ATTITUDE OF ACCEPTANCE

In business, acceptance becomes a huge challenge because failure is most often not an option. The impact of failure can be far-reaching. A product sales target not met can adversely impact many stakeholders, including investors and shareholders. This becomes a major source of stress, especially for business leaders.

The problem is, we tend to think of acceptance too simplistically. The first misconception that people hold is that a mindful person should have no expectations. However, this expectation of not having an expectation is itself unreasonable and goes against our fundamental nature. Expectations are nothing but desire by another name. Every minute, we desire to do and experience something. Desire is the glory of our species. With desire, we created great innovations and technologies, overcame challenges and advanced human civilisation. Without desire, human beings would have gone extinct. We innately desire. Hence, not to have expectations is not possible.

The issue, therefore, is not with expectations but how we deal with the results. For example, how do you accept the outcome of projects you are accountable for? Sometimes the projects you lead are successful and sometimes they are not. Or they fall short of the intended outcome, perhaps even becoming the cause of your losing your job.

Every action has four possible outcomes:

1. Succeeded

2. Exceeded the success criteria

3. Failed to meet the success criteria

4. Created a radical negative outcome

In mindfulness we are interested in noticing our mental responses to each of these four outcomes. It is quite usual that we are happy when we meet or exceed our success criteria, and become sad or depressed with the other two outcomes. While we do not want to take away the emotions associated with these outcomes, the important question to ask is whether we accept the results with equanimity.

Here is where the second misconnection about acceptance arises. People tend to assume that acceptance leads to non-action. That is not so. In every one of the four outcomes, there is an imperative to act. But what we need is the equanimity to accept any one of the four without a knee-jerk reaction. This is required in leadership because most of the time we celebrate the first two outcomes and order a firing squad for the other two.

In summary, acceptance is all about developing the ability to be equanimous and accommodating in any of the four outcomes before we respond. It is more of a psychological trait than a practice. This trait is developed through mindfulness practices.

ACCEPTANCE

* * *

We have now covered the heart of MIL, which is the *being* stage of mindfulness practices. In this stage we discussed Awareness, Attention and Acceptance. We now move on to the *doing* stage of MIL, starting with Action.

Action

One of the most important aspects of leadership is action. While we are practising mindfulness, it does not mean that we are in a permanent state of being. In fact, for a leader, *doing* is as important as *being*, with the key difference being that a mindful leader is able to see the intimate non-separation between the two.

What do I mean by non-separation? The relationship between being and doing is an interesting one. They are not completely independent, yet they are also not mutually dependent. Doing depends on being, but being does not necessarily depend on doing. This relationship is key to MIL as we act from mindfulness and its practices and insights. It is mindfulness practices that inform action, not the other way round.

In most mindfulness discourses, action is not a big subject compared to being. However, as leaders, we need to act. We need to increase profits, sustain profitability, reduce costs, hire talent, develop people, enhance quality, give direction, innovate, etc. All of these tasks require you to *do*.

Leadership, according to Paul Hersey and Ken Blanchard, is "a process of influencing individual or group activities in efforts toward achieving organisational objectives in a given situation". This requires not just being, but doing as well. As with most enterprises, we move from ideation to implementation. Having developed awareness, attention and acceptance, it is imperative that we take action.

In all this, we must be careful not to create a chasm between doing and being. Instead, allow the doing to arise from being. Action then becomes a response rather than a reaction.

RESPONSABILITY

The ability to respond requires a good anchor in being. The reactionary state, which is a symptom of autopilot mode, is what we need to beware of as leaders. Reactions lack awareness, acceptance and attention. Mindfulness helps us leaders by being anchored in "ResponsAbility", which is a key trait of mindful leaders.

I define responsability as the ability to respond. Mindfulness helps us develop this ability and helps us to perform wholesome actions as leaders. Wholesome actions are actions that keep in focus the well-being of the people, the organisation/team and the society. We can practise wholesome actions at the level of the self, as well as on an organisational scale. The idea is to bring out the best in humanity and create positive change.

At this point, you may wonder if such a thing as a perfect response exists. The answer is yes and no. A perfect response exists only as a best possible response at a given time, place and circumstance. The same response may not be relevant in another time, place and circumstance. Responses are always relative. We need to take into account the changing landscapes in which we operate, and yet we need to respond from a space of relative changelessness which is our being.

INTENTION VS INSTINCT

The next important aspect of action for a mindful leader is the value of clear intention. This intention is based on the insights gained from mindfulness practices. It is the clear recognition that humans seek happiness, well-being and wholesomeness in their lives.

Quite the opposite of clear intention is instinct. Instinct is the reaction of our brain based on stored impressions and the involuntary reaction to stimuli. When instinct is not tamed by clear intention, it can be provocative, regrettable and even destructive.

Animals primarily behave based on instinct and we humans do share some of these instincts. These include seeking food, sex, sleep and reacting to fear. All of these instincts appear to stem from the amygdala – they are in a way our programmed needs.

While all of us operate from these instincts, it is important that we do not allow our behaviours and responses be a consequence of these instincts. Hence, intention rather than instinct is required for mindful leaders, such that our decisions, strategies and goals are born of clear intention rooted in happiness, well-being and wholesomeness.

WELL-BEING FOCUS

As leaders, the well-being of our team is one of our foremost concerns. I remember an incident where I had to fire one of my staff as a result of discipline issues. I had several discussions with him and offered to counsel and guide him through the difficulties he was facing. He was given countless opportunities to revert to his prior good performance. However, it came to a point where the well-being of the department was adversely affected and our performance was at stake. In the end, it was decided amicably that he had to leave in the best interests of both his own well-being and that of the department.

It is quite often the case that when a staff underperforms or is unable to deliver results, both the organisation and the individual suffer. It is only right that we set a clear intention as to what is needed in such situations.

Well-being is always an effect of wholesomeness. That is why change in business and leadership, too, has to be wholesome. Some people say that business models are changing and we need to embrace this change, especially as we are entering the fourth industrial revolution. However, it is not innovation that we are looking for in new business models but wholesomeness, because innovation without wholesomeness is of no use to humanity. I will talk more about this in the chapter on wisdom.

EFFECTUATION WITH DISCRETION

The next important attribute of action is the ability to execute intentions with discretion. A year ago, as I was jogging in the park near my home, I saw a man carrying a few clear plastic bags with what looked like goldfish in them. He was standing on a bridge, and appeared to be opening up the bags and preparing to pour the fish into the river. This practice is quite popular in Asian countries where some people purchase live birds, fishes and other aquatic animals from pet shops for the purpose of releasing them into their "natural" habitat as a symbolic act of liberation.

The man at the bridge was clearly in the process of doing this, except that the bridge was a good five metres above the surface of the river, and a drop from that height could easily kill the fish. The man had a clear intention but the effectuation was way off the mark. Action requires discretion.

Sometimes as leaders we do not pay sufficient attention to effectuation and discretion. How we effect an intention is as important as the intention itself. Paying attention means noticing the executive aspects of ideas and the results. There is a tendency to assume that the end justifies the means. I would say that this is not true except in dire or exceptional situations. As mindful leaders, we should bring our awareness to the entire chain of intention, action and results.

BEHAVIOUR VS INTENTION

Another common misconception is the notion that mindful leaders are measured by their behaviour. Because we often judge a person by their behaviour, we have this belief that behaviour is equal to the person. We judge people by their actions and form an impression based on those actions. However, that is not true.

One of the key motivators of behaviour is intention. A single intention can induce two different actions; a single type of action can be due to two different intentions. A hangman takes the life of a murderer. Both the murderer and the hangman have taken a life, but one is seen to have done the right thing and the other wrong. This is a classic illustration of the same action with two different intentions.

Hence, behaviours can be diverse for the same intention. This could happen in leadership, where team members notice these inconsistencies and form a judgment of the leader. It is imperative that leaders cultivate an inquiring culture, where team members feel safe to inquire into intention rather than judge the behaviour. Leaders should also communicate their intentions more clearly to their team members.

Mindful leaders are more than what they do, and not limited by it. Intention completes the picture. That is the reason why behaviour should not be the sole basis for judgment.

KNOWER-DOER CONFLICT

As we keep noticing our actions and thoughts, we may also start noticing the "knower-doer conflict", commonly known as cognitive dissonance.

I have encountered leaders who believe in positivity, objectivity and the need for conversations during conflict, and they promote this approach within their team. However, when a conflict situation does arise, these leaders fail to confer and communicate; instead, they make private decisions and only thereafter inform their team members.

This illustrates well the gap between knowing and doing. In the domain of knowing, we are usually fully aware of the knowledge and values we possess. When the weather is fair, we find it easy to talk about these values and to put them into practice. But when the weather is bad, we do the exact opposite!

How do we align our doing with our knowing? One of the best ways is to strengthen our prefrontal cortex – this is the part of our brain that is responsible for executive functions. Mindfulness empowers this part of our brain. As I started practising mindfulness, I found it easier to follow up on what I promised, to be consistent in my actions, to execute according to my values and knowledge, all the way down to seemingly trivial things like not pressing the snooze button on my alarm clock as frequently as I used to.

* * *

As you would have inferred by now, what is required of action is for it to be informed by your mindfulness practices. Without mindfulness practices, action could become arbitrary or biased. The interplay of action and mindfulness practices is only conscious as long as it is practised. With continuous practice, mindfulness becomes a trait, and doing effortlessly arises from being.

Attitude

Mindfulness-Informed Leadership can never become meaningful and valuable without discussing the conventional expectations of leadership in the changing world that we live in.

There are many definitions of leadership. John Maxwell has stated that "leadership is all influence", while Paul Hersey and Ken Blanchard define it as "a process of influencing individual or group activities in efforts toward achieving organisational objectives in a given situation". I personally love Nancy Adler's definition, that leaders are "people whose vision, courage, and influence set ideas, people, organisation and societies in motion toward the betterment of their organisation, their community and the world".

In these definitions and many others, one key concept that appears to be common to all leaders is "influence". Apart from that, it seems there is no single leadership model that applies to the whole of humanity.

Leadership authors and gurus have identified as many as 120 leadership competencies. Tiina Jokinen from the University of Vaasa classifies core leadership competencies into three broad groups: self-awareness; engagement in personal transformation; and inquisitiveness. Indeed, these three macro competencies are closely related to mindfulness practices.

LEADERSHIP TRADITIONS

I have spent some time looking at ancient business and commercial literature related indirectly to contemplative traditions, going as far back as two thousand years. And I have found that there are specific trends that demonstrate the timeless nature of business and leadership.

All cultures from ancient times have considered ethics, or values, vital components of leadership. These values include honesty, justice and even discretionary action. They are enshrined, explicitly and implicitly, in almost all theories of leadership today, and embodied in the leaders we look up to.

At the same time, however, changes in our environment and our needs exert a force in the opposite direction. There is a tendency for us to sacrifice timeless fundamental values as a result of elevating our time-relative responses.

I see the potential for mindfulness to pave the way for the re-discovery of what is innate and natural to human leadership.

In mindfulness, we do not create a chasm between timeless values and relative values. Looking at the leaders of humanity over thousands of years, we can see in them values that remained timeless and relevant at all times as well as values that were responses to emergent needs. This is natural. What mindfulness does is to create more opportunities to find what is already in us, what belongs to whole of humanity.

My mindfulness work with educational institutions and large corporations has been primarily aimed at bringing this philosophy into their physical and mind spaces. Google, Intel, Aetna and General

Mills have all gone big on mindfulness, generating measurable impact. I wish more leaders did the same.

SELF-DIRECTEDNESS AND SELF-INTEREST

There are certain attitudinal traits that help us in cultivating ourselves as mindful leaders. One of these is self-directedness, a trait that all of us have within us – in varying degrees. It is the sense of pro-action that arises in certain conditions and situations. As much as individuals vary in their propensity for it, it is definitely a key ingredient in leadership. While we may be dependent on others and on extraneous factors for our success, it is important to recognise that it is in self-directedness that a leader shapes his vision. Instead of reacting to situations, a self-directed leader responds in need as well as anticipates what is needed from his wisdom.

Self-interest is a much-debated trait in leadership discussions. People tend to think that great leaders are those who place themselves first in times of adversity and place their members first when times are good. I beg to differ from this conclusion from a philosophical standpoint although I agree with it generally.

I am totally for leaders who are altruistic as such traits tug at our heartstrings. However, one of the key discussions in the wisdom traditions of mindfulness is that it is impossible to be absolutely selfless in our thoughts and action. The reason is that self-interest cannot be removed from any sane human mind. All desires and intentions are premised on self-interest.

For example, two leaders took different approaches to achieving cost reduction. One decided to do it through lay-offs, while the other decided to find placements in other companies through an agent at the organisation's expense. Both of these leaders would feel the same degree of inner resolution or consummation having accomplished their goals. One felt good because his self-interest was to achieve his goal of reducing cost; the interest of the other leader was to ensure that the future of his staff was a happy one. In the process, both of them only satisfied their own interests.

So the discussion of self-interest as regards leadership is somewhat futile. Rather, what needs to be reflected on is how well wisdom has permeated these thoughts, words and actions. In my life, I have met many leaders who have been selfless in the conventional sense of the word without recognising the fact that all of us are actually just solving our own problems in the process.

LEADERSHIP COMPASS

Leading with mindfulness is ideally facilitative in nature rather than prescriptive. Your leadership uses awareness as its compass. A compass never tells you anything about the destination. All that it does is to show you the direction. But a compass is of no use without a destination. Mindfulness enters the picture here, creating an acute awareness of the "hows" and "whys" behind your goals and purpose.

I beg to differ with those pop leadership theories that prescribe indiscretionary and intention-centred goals and purpose – a sort of misconstrued stepchild of facilitation in business. In this school of thought, a person defines and takes a journey entirely based on his sense of values, knowledge and goal. Facilitators and coaches are usually impartial to these goals, while the growing coaching field provides yet more fodder for such beliefs.

In mindfulness, this belief is challenged because it gives total empowerment to people who think that they are fully capable of making wise decisions instead of seeing wisdom as a work in progress. I have always wondered what an executive coach would have done with Adolf Hitler if he had sought executive coaching services to annihilate the Jewish population. Can you see the absurdity of impartiality in leadership?

The uniqueness of mindfulness is that we are not only interested in the process of reaching a goal but also the goal itself. The means are as important as the end. The end has to be wholesome in every sense of the word. I have always liked the metaphor of our shadows. No matter what time of the day it may be, your shadow on the ground will always remain rooted to your feet. Likewise, your leadership thoughts, words and actions will always be rooted in wholesomeness. This is the kind of anchor that is required of a mindful leader.

INQUIRY-CENTRED

Another very important attitudinal trait of MIL is the spirit of inquiry. This is closely related to one of the core competencies of global leadership as mentioned above: inquisitiveness.

Questions and curiosity are important tools in inquiry-centred leadership. Obviously I am not referring to the sort of fault-finding investigation and interrogation that we undertake when things do not turn out the way we intended. I remember, for instance, a senior leader in my career who was always very quick to find a sacrificial lamb for any issue that smeared his reputation.

Rather, inquiry-centred behaviour is concerned with genuinely finding out what happened or what is. It does not pre-occupy itself with the future or the past but understands the past and future without a sense of remorse or anxiety. In fact, the past and the future are only referenced on the present.

But in the world of business, how can we possibly avoid thinking about the future? As managers and leaders, we have to plan ahead, to consider the future of our businesses, to sustain long-term profitability. In fact, even in our personal lives, so much of our thoughts and actions are focused on the future, from buying insurance for ourselves to providing for our children.

The mindful way of dealing with this is to understand that it is not the future and the past that create problems but the emotions associated with them. The past evokes remorse, resentment, non-acceptance, etc., while the future evokes anxiety, excitement, hope, etc. All of these feelings and emotions severely impair your objectivity if you are unable to accept them. That is what we are dealing with here. To address the past and future mindfully in the present, we can only do so if we are not derailed by our emotions.

BEING A LEADER, NOT BECOMING ONE

The other thing that leadership manuals do is to make you want to "become" a leader. This is especially emphasised when you take up the reins of a leader for the first time. It leaves you "wanting".

Some leadership theories and frameworks spend a lot of time on "becoming" and on achieving a set of desired leadership traits. They push you towards excessive experimentation and the learning of skills to become a better leader. These keep you in the *doing* mode.

Doing and being are both necessary. It is like learning to ride a bicycle. First, you set an intention to ride it effectively. Then, what you should be doing is to ride the bicycle until you glide into the art of balancing. You do not learn it by studying the bicycle and its mechanics or reading a book. You need to actually ride the bicycle. You need to pay attention in the present moment without letting the future image of competent riding distract you. You just ride, ride and keep riding. Everything is done in the present moment. Thereafter you move on to riding the bicycle on different terrains to gain incremental mastery.

Similarly, in leadership we do need to learn as well as practise, while paying attention to what needs to be done in the present moment with a clear intention. You lead, lead and keep leading. By doing that, you are always *being* a leader and ever a work in progress.

The *being* mode of leadership can also be understood through a clock analogy. It is easy to notice the second hand of the clock as it moves every second. The minute hand can also be seen to move with keener attention. But the movement of the hour hand is very difficult to notice and pay attention to. You only notice it after it has moved. The being of leadership is like the hour hand: you notice the difference in retrospect, not while it's happening.

But there is a catch to this approach, and that is time. We often set targets against time, including leadership development. MIL does not work well if leadership development is urgent. MIL is about sustaining and creating change at the level of traits, not state. It takes time, and that is the reason why present-moment attention is crucial. Radical and quick changes are usually not sustainable. That's why mindfulness-informed interventions are usually taught over a span of eight weeks.

The other drawback of leadership development with urgent action plans is that it may submerge you into a perennial "becoming" or "doing" mode instead of focusing on the present moment. Leaders who continuously "become" stifle their members and throw them into confusion because the latter just do not know who their leaders are as the leaders keep changing too fast and too radically. The sense of "becoming" needs to resolve into "being" with self-awareness. Leading mindfully is all about understanding this process of simultaneous being and doing, although the being takes precedence.

In fact, the change is already happening as you read this book, because knowledge informs awareness. Both being and doing lead to wisdom, and wisdom changes your attitude naturally. You are not waiting for something to happen.

SIMPLICITY

Simplicity is the ultimate sophistication.
— Leonardo da Vinci

Sometimes, in our attempt to come across more sophisticated, we tend to complicate simple matters when what is needed is simplicity. For example, think of how academic research papers are often written in a way that the layman cannot understand. That same knowledge can be successfully communicated to a layman provided we think from the standpoint of simplicity.

I was once engaged by a school principal to teach mindfulness to all the teachers. However, the school leadership team was excluded from the session as they had something more important to attend to. During the workshop, I asked the teachers how well they were doing in the areas of values and outcomes. Interestingly, the younger teachers, who happened to be millennials, were rather unhappy with the way things were. A couple of them said they did not have a sense of involvement in the school's strategic direction. After this, I led them all through some value reflections and a couple of mindfulness practices.

When the workshop ended, the principal came by the room and browsed through the points that had been written on the flipcharts. Her eyes immediately fell on the areas that the teachers had voiced their unhappiness about. She wanted to know who (not what) contributed to it. She also wanted to know who the unhappy teachers were. In the process she became upset herself.

From a mindfulness perspective, the issue was quite simple and could have been solved simply by having a conversation with all the teachers non-judgmentally and finding out what was needed. Instead, it appeared to me that the principal was heading in the direction of a witch hunt.

* * *

We have thus far looked at the traits of MIL, which are its attitudinal foundations. These attitudes are cultivated by mindfulness practices followed by Action and finally the Wisdom that arises as a result of it. Without personal mindfulness practices, one may find it very difficult to be a mindful leader who by nature delivers from awareness, acceptance and attention.

However, many mindful leaders may not even know of mindfulness as a practice. So how can we consider them mindful leaders? This has got to do with personality traits. People can exhibit trait mindfulness or dispositional mindfulness without any mindfulness practices. I have worked with leaders who are naturally endowed with these traits. Their personal values, upbringing and adult experiences could have induced mindful attitudes in them. So in a sense it is not necessary to practise mindfulness in order to be a mindful leader.

However, I would say that this is the exception and not the norm. You should not walk away assuming that you are mindful but rather use the principles in MIL to find resonance and sustain it consciously. I would recommend people with dispositional mindfulness to practise mindfulness to continue being aware of your being, and to be conscious role models for your team members.

Wisdom

The final domain of MIL is wisdom. Human beings are called *Homo sapiens* for a reason. The word *sapiens* means wisdom. This is indeed one of the most defining characteristics of the human species. Our capacity to process knowledge and experience is what makes us unique and different from other living beings.

I define wisdom as the assimilated knowledge that the Self, others and the world are connected. Wisdom is humanistic and responds in a way that promotes well-being and realises wholeness. It is the culmination of mindfulness practices and action, and impacts attitude. It cannot be forced or faked. It is dispositional and yet can be practised as a sustained value with conscious effort in the domains of being and doing.

WISDOM FROM MINDFULNESS

There are two kinds of wisdom. One is called esoteric wisdom and the other humanistic wisdom. Esoteric wisdom is that which is understood only by a few and more often than not it is born of religious or philosophical inspiration. The rare few who possess esoteric wisdom usually live a highly eudaimonic life.

Humanistic wisdom, on the other hand, is the wisdom born of conscious insights and realisable through self-effort. This is the wisdom we are interested in and which is relevant to MIL. In this book, when I use the word "wisdom", I am referring to humanistic wisdom.

The world-renowned psychologist Robert Sternberg defines wisdom as that which seeks the common good through the use of tacit knowledge and values with a balance of Self and others. This definition is consistent with what mindfulness culminates in. As per my earlier definition, I consider wisdom as the insights born of "assimilated" knowledge about oneself, others and the world. Wisdom allows you to recognise the connection among the three.

I would recognise a wise person when his thoughts, feelings and actions arise from his being. A wise person views himself as a whole being and acts with wholesomeness. He appreciates the fundamental human desire to be whole, complete and happy.

While wisdom is not needed to lead an organisation or a team, it can make leadership more effective and inspiring. Wise leaders place importance on the means and ends of business; they are acutely aware of the impact that their leadership has on every stakeholder of the business.

One of the ways that mindfulness helps to realise wisdom is by acting as a catalyst for focusing our attention on the realities of life, as we discussed in the chapter on Attention. While there are certainly many paths to realising wisdom, mindfulness is perhaps one of the easiest and most regulated.

The second role that mindfulness plays in the realisation of wisdom is in the mode of inquiry and introspection. As Socrates said, "True wisdom comes to each of us when we realise how little we understand about life, ourselves, and the world around us." This gives rise to humility and keeps us always curious and inquiring.

The third role of mindfulness practices, along with action, is in generating insights. As we practise mindfulness, we start to see things more clearly through the insights generated through our thoughts, emotions and actions.

There is also a connection between knowledge and wisdom. They are quite different things, as you would have already inferred from the discussions, but yet connected. Wisdom depends on knowledge but the presence of knowledge may not necessarily mean the presence of wisdom. So the first step into the world of wisdom is indeed through knowledge. But it is inquiry and introspection that help in leading to wisdom. Mindfulness again makes curiosity and inquiry the bedrock of all its practices.

Knowing what wisdom is one thing, but knowing what it is not is also important. There is a possibility that wisdom can lead to megalomania and narcissism. Sternberg has proposed six fallacies of wisdom which I find very revealing. Wisdom, according to him, is not:

- Egocentric – An egocentric leader thinks and acts in ways that only benefit himself as he considers himself to be wiser than others.

- Unrealistically optimistic – Such a leader holds on to the belief that everything will turn out right because he thinks he knows better, or knows nature better.

- Omniscient – A wise leader will not fancy himself omniscient, i.e., all-knowing and hence infallible. He knows that there is always more to know.

- Omnipotent – A wise leader won't think that he can do anything he wants, or assume that the whole organisation or team is at his disposal.

- Invulnerable – A wise leader will not make the assumption that his wisdom can overcome vulnerability.

- Ethically disengaged – A wise leader will not consider himself to be beyond the ethical considerations that apply to other people. Being ethically disengaged is a classic trait of religious leaders who think they are above the law.

Knowing what wisdom is not helps us recognise the wisdom in us.

WHOLENESS AND WHOLESOMENESS

Wholeness is not a destination, a place like nirvana
that we arrive at and simply stay in. It is dynamic,
with different levels, much like a spiral. We experience
wholeness in the moment in everyday life, because
now is all we have.
— Wendy Tan

Wisdom recognises wholeness and the value of being wholesome. With wisdom, we recognise that wholeness is not a state to be attained but a way of being. You are whole in the present moment. Your being is always whole. That said, most of us find it easier to see ourselves as seeking wholeness. Everyone you meet is either seeking this wholeness unconsciously or consciously.

Wholesomeness is about acting towards achieving well-being in every aspect of an individual and the world we live in. A mindful leader sees this value very clearly from within, without any external motivation. It is not just about doing things right, but doing the right thing as well.

With wisdom, we recognise that our employees, members, owners, customers, shareholders, suppliers, creditors, society and other stakeholders are after all people just like us. All of them are seeking this wholeness through so many endeavours, ideas, activities, relationships, etc. Recognising this universal fact allows us to respond with compassion. All our actions are prompted from this space of wisdom when we stay anchored as mindful leaders.

BEING WISE

As you would have inferred by now, wisdom is the culmination of attitude, mindfulness practices and action. Mindfulness cannot be practised in a cave. It requires active interaction with the world in the present. The place where you are is the place where you are meant to be and that is where you experiment. Your home, workplace and the society you live in is your mindfulness gym. This is where you practise MIL.

Coming back to the diagram below, we now appreciate that the relationship between the six domains of MIL is not sequential. We don't move linearly from, say, attitude to wisdom. That is not the case with MIL. At any given time, all of us have our attitudes, and are performing actions with a certain degree of wisdom even without mindfulness in our lives.

The only aspect that is perhaps not in our lives at this moment is that of mindfulness practices. The moment we start practising mindfulness, the other domains are immediately energised. This happens instantaneously and evolves on its own as you deepen your mindfulness practices.

SUMMARY

We have now examined the case for Mindfulness-Informed Leadership as well as the change it can potentially create in your leadership, team and organisational culture. We have discovered what MIL is and how we can stay rooted being a mindful leader. We have also explored the six domains of MIL in detail.

Now it is time for us to delve into a 56-day leadership journey that will take you into the deeper aspects of MIL. These 56 insights have been distilled from my personal journey as a leader, manager, supervisor, worker and most importantly, as a simple human being. They will expand on the mindfulness domains, so that you find resonance in your being and doing.

The 56-Day Leadership Journey

Thank you for coming this far with me. From this point onwards, we will be taking an 8-week journey into deepening Mindfulness-Informed Leadership (MIL). In this part of the book, you will find 56 Insights and 8 Mindfulness Practices to strengthen your practice and appreciation of MIL.

Please treat these 56 insights like seeds placed in your awareness. Just as seeds of the same species of plant grow differently depending on the quality of the soil where they were planted, availability of sunlight, climate and environment, likewise these 56 seeds of insight will germinate and flourish differently in different minds. No two mindful leaders will be the same, yet they share the same understanding of mindfulness.

As you read these insights, remember that you are not obliged to agree with them. It is perfectly fine for you to disagree. Accept this, as the intention is not to indoctrinate you but purely to inform your awareness.

I would not recommend that you speed-read this part of the book to finish it as soon as you can. The purpose behind the design of the insights is to allow the mind to notice its habits and to absorb one insight a day. The eight mindfulness practices are also paced such that you practise one technique for seven days before moving on to the next one.

Consider setting aside 10–15 minutes a day to read this part of the book over eight weeks. I would like you to notice your mental responses without any form of judgment as you maintain this tempo of one insight a day. At the same time, I am mindful that I do not want to make this a rule. This is my recommendation. Do what works for you – mindfully.

At times these insights may inspire you to stop, start or continue doing something. Or a new insight may arise as you read. Do take note of these thoughts and behaviours and reflect on them before you act.

At the end of each insight there will be a couple of Inquiry questions. These questions are an opportunity for you to inquire into the assimilation of the topic and its relevance to you as a leader.

WEEK 1 MINDFULNESS PRACTICE

BODY SCAN

Purpose

Get in touch with your body and "listen" to its feedback, train your attention, and release emotions that may be stored in your body.

Method

The body scan is practised by bringing attention to different parts of your body in turn. You start by bringing attention to your right big toe and then to the other toes. Then slowly move on to the sole of your foot, ankle, shin, calf muscles and so on, all the way to the top of your head.

- First, ensure you are in an environment where you have the least external distraction.
- Lie down on an exercise mat or a flat surface comfortably with your eyes closed.
- Start your practice by mentally noticing the different parts of your body.
- Prepare a sequence based on the sections of your body, for example: left leg, right leg, back of the torso, front of the torso, left arm, right arm, neck, face, back of the head.
- Start noticing each of these sections of your body for a minute or 30 seconds before moving on to the next section. In order not to watch the time during your practice, wait till you've completed the entire body scan before you look at how much time you took altogether and adjust your pace in your next practice.

1

JUDGMENT AND NON-JUDGMENT

One of the biggest challenges for a mindful leader is how to reconcile the attitude of non-judgment observed during mindfulness practices with having to make judgments at work. Appraisals, evaluations, decisions – these are some of the common occasions when we are called upon to make judgments. Does this seem antithetical to the attitude of inviting and accepting experiences non-judgmentally which is a hallmark of all mindfulness practices?

While we cannot avoid making judgments as leaders, what we can do is to pay attention to the type of judgments we make. Often our judgments are influenced by many subjective factors – our values, likes and dislikes, biases, preferences and personality traits. As mindful leaders, what we want is to make objective judgments that help us view things *as they are*.

One of the ways this can be done is to isolate any issue at hand from the people associated with it. In doing so, we avoid passing judgments on the people, and instead focus our thoughts on the issue itself. When subsequently reviewing the matter with the people involved, try to focus on the behaviours that might have caused the issue rather than penalising the whole person.

An important insight for mindful leaders is recognising that the judgments we make are relative, not absolute. Relative judgments are bound by time, place and circumstance. They are necessary for our day-to-day functioning, from crossing a road to choosing a life partner. The validity of a relative judgements is never absolute. For example, a person deemed to be incompetent at a particular task may not always be incompetent, in a different time, different place or under different circumstances.

In the business context, judgments relating to business strategy, mission and core values are all relative. They do not stand the test of time and environment. This is precisely why businesses review their strategy annually and re-strategise every three years or so. A mindful leader does not mistake business "truths" for absolute truths.

Objectivity in judgment is further cultivated by being aware of generalisations. As human beings we are prone to making generalisations because they give us the illusion that we have found a timeless truth. Statements such as "Men are aggressive" and "Women are emotional" appeal to us as expedient rules of thumb, but we should be mindful they can potentially cloud our objectivity.

Only in a space of non-judgment do people feel comfortable speaking the truth. If your team members feel judged for raising difficult issues, they may prefer to keep quiet, or tell you something that is sweet to your ears rather than the truth. This can lead to grave consequences for your team and your organisation as a whole.

Hence, whether in meetings, conversations or presentations, we should be aware of our prejudices and the way we express our thoughts. Allow people to express their full thoughts before scrutinising them objectively.

Inquiry

1. Do I generalise my observations? Do I review them from time to time?
2. Do people around me share their honest views with me or do they share what I like to hear?

2

THE IMPORTANCE OF FEEDBACK

We all need people who will
give us feedback.
— Bill Gates

In today's business world, leaders are encouraged to give and receive feedback. While giving feedback as leaders is common, receiving feedback seems to be a taboo. That's because leaders are viewed as infallible creatures who are never wanting. As leaders, we assume such a persona because that is what is expected.

However, receiving feedback is so very important for a leader. Feedback reveals a lot about our blind self and hidden self (refer back to the Awareness chapter). Without hearing feedback, we do not know how our actions and behaviours are received by others.

It can, of course, be difficult to accept "negative" feedback. The mind tends to instinctively deflect such feedback and defend itself against the perceived criticism. That is because the mind wishes to be perfect, spotless and error-free. Feedback is seen as room for improvement.

The biggest challenge, therefore, lies in receiving feedback without self-judgment. With mindfulness, we realise that it is not about the feedback per se, but the mental reaction that takes place when feedback is received.

The mindful leader pays attention to his mental response to feedback rather than leaping into action. Not all feedback requires action. The desire to act often stems from self-judgment. Your autopilot wants you to be seen favourably in the eyes of your team members, hence urging you into action. Perhaps you received a customer complaint or feedback from an internal stakeholder. You assume that action is immediately required, but that may not be so. Some feedback may only call for reflection. In making your response, it is of utmost importance that you are aware of the intention behind it.

The same goes for positive feedback. We love positive feedback as it tells us that people regard our leadership favourably. But I would urge you to notice how your mind reacts to positive feedback the same way as with negative feedback. Try noticing any difference with attention and non-judgment, and do not rush to act or feel disproportionately self-satisfied.

When giving feedback, it is good to note that people who value eudaimonia (refer back to the chapter on Attention) may brush off your feedback rather lightly or take it too seriously. The former reaction could be due to a deeply entrenched conviction in their purpose, while the latter could be due to their intense desire to discover purpose. Giving feedback to highly eudaimonic team members thus poses a challenge to leaders, and should be done with this understanding in mind.

Inquiry

1. How do I look at myself when negative feedback is given to me either directly or indirectly?
2. Am I comfortable accepting my imperfections?

3

WORDS CREATE WORLDS

Language has been the subject of a great deal of discussion in ancient and modern thought. Words are seen as a means of creating knowledge. Whether spoken or written, they have the unique ability to communicate knowledge about things known and unknown, which may eventually transform into wisdom.

Words also have the power to induce emotions. Words such as "weep", "murder" and "regret" have strong emotions associated with them, which are triggered when we encounter, hear or read them. On the other hand, words such as "joy", "celebrate" and "love" evoke a whole different set of emotions.

So the usage of words can create vastly different worlds. Saying "I am stupid" is quite different from saying "I am ignorant". A statement like "The strategy is weak" has a different effect from "The strategy needs to be robust". One's choice of words can be very powerful in either inspiring change or forcing change.

The discretionary use of words is a crucial part of leadership behaviour. What we say as leaders can inspire our team to action or kill their spirit. I have seen leaders who repeatedly spew remarks that denigrate and demoralise their team members. This can have a huge detrimental effect on your leadership. Because this is an abuse of power and trust. On the other hand, a leader who chooses his words carefully has the potential to bring out the best in people.

Even a simple case of using "we" instead of "you" can make a big difference. Words such as "you" and "I" are very personal, and can cloud the issue at hand, in addition to making people feel targeted and blamed. The same goes for asking "Why...?" questions when something has gone wrong. Using words such as "we" and "us" instead can help to objectify the issue, allowing all parties to reflect and move ahead productively.

The other thing to note about words is that the same words in different settings or cultures can have different meanings and connotations. The first floor is not the ground floor in some countries. And a cider is not always a non-alcoholic drink. Assuming that words are interpreted uniformly in all contexts can become a stumbling block for leaders.

Inquiry

1. What emotions do I want more of in my members?
2. What is my intention behind questions that start with a "Why"?

4

PURPOSE AND MEANING

Discussion of purpose and meaning has become very popular in business these days. People who have a clear purpose are seen to outperform people who don't. It is almost impossible to appreciate purpose and meaning in business or leadership without understanding purpose and meaning in life.

First, we need to distinguish between these three phrases:

1. Purpose of life
2. Purpose in life
3. Meaning in life

Purpose of life is not often discussed in secular contexts but found in abundance in spiritual and religious literature. Examining all these constructs and beliefs, a common thread appears: All of us, regardless of our religious or secular affiliations, seek happiness. It is as if we are innately made for the experience of happiness. It seems safe, therefore, to conclude that happiness is the purpose of life.

Here is a story. A rich businessman once visited a remote village, in which his parents had grown up. In the village he met a fisherman who went out fishing every day in his small boat. He would catch a couple of fish, and sell them in the local market, making enough for his subsistence. One day, the businessman took a ride on the fisherman's boat to cross the river. He asked the fisherman about his business:

Businessman: How long do you work a day?

Fisherman: Three hours.

Businessman: If you worked longer hours, could you catch more fish?

Fisherman: Yes. But what for?

Businessman: So that you can buy more boats.

Fisherman: And then?

Businessman: Then you could employ others in the village and make more money.

Fisherman: And then?

Businessman: Then you could buy a bigger house, cars and make investments.

Fisherman: What for?

Businessman: So that you can be happy!

Fisherman: I am already happy.

This leads us to the second point, purpose in life. The businessman and the fisherman both sought happiness, but in different ways. While the purpose *of* life was the same for both of them, their purpose *in* life was different.

Purpose in life is something we may not have thought much about. The element of self-actualisation in Maslow's hierarchy of needs is interpreted to be the purpose in life. All of us define this differently based on our perspective of life, life experiences and beliefs. You may consider your purpose in life to be serving others, while someone else might consider his purpose of life to be the exact opposite, that is, utilising the strengths of others.

Meaning in life has a very strong connection to purpose in life. In fact, they influence each other. Sometimes these two terms are used interchangeably. Our values, goals and mission are what constitute meaning. And these can significantly influence our purpose in life. Always remember that your team members may have their own sets of purpose and meaning in life – very likely not even related to work.

In mindfulness we are very careful not to make the search for purpose and meaning another goal because it is not a requirement that everyone needs to know this to be functional. People who lack even physical and economic security may not think about these questions. So it is important that we focus on the living rather than the searching. The search for meaning can rob you of the very happiness you are looking for.

So, instead of going on an active quest for your purpose and meaning, park that desire in your mind and practise mindfulness, through which you may then come to an awareness of what brings meaning to your life and your leadership.

Inquiry

1. What part of my life makes me happy?
2. Do I know what makes my team members happy?

5

PURPOSEFUL AND MEANINGFUL LEADERSHIP

What is your purpose in leadership? What made you become a leader? Did you have a choice? Were you prepared? Think about these questions for a few minutes before you proceed.

Building on the previous day's insight, let us discuss the difference between the purpose *of* leadership and purpose *in* leadership. The former is universal and applicable to all leaders while the latter is personal and in fact optional.

There are leaders who have integrated the two, devoting their whole life to their leadership. Steve Jobs, one of the greatest innovators and leaders of our age, said that he wrote his autobiography because "I wasn't always there for [my children], and I wanted them to know why". He saw, on hindsight perhaps, that his work at Apple took him away from his children, and there was no way for him to buy back all the lost time. Leaders like Jobs have a great impact on their organisations and even on society, but they often sacrifice a lot of themselves in the process. Is this a sacrifice you would be comfortable making?

In mindfulness we prefer to view leadership as just another role we take on in life – a role that is dependent on your being – rather than equating the role with your being.

Try not to compare yourself with leaders or people who claim to be self-actualised or to have realised happiness. It's not a competition. I always emphasise that the value of self-actualisation is in the living, just like the value of a joke is in the laughter. It is not a subject or a theory. That is the reason why in mindfulness we allow meaning and purpose to arise from mindfulness practices rather than actively hunting for it.

If you find your leadership purpose, all well and good; but if you don't, that's fine too. Contrary to the popularity of "purposeful leadership" in current literature, finding your leadership purpose is entirely optional. It is a bonus, not a requirement.

As Klaus Schwab says in his book *The Fourth Industrial Revolution,* it will be increasingly difficult to achieve fulfilment through our work in the future. We need to manage ourselves in being pragmatic and realistic instead of putting undue pressure on ourselves to become an "idealised" leader.

Inquiry

1. Do I see myself as someone bigger than my leadership role?
2. How much time do I devote to the other roles in my life?

6

THE DIAMOND PRINCIPLE

Many of the leaders I have worked with tell me that effecting change in an organisation is invariably an uphill, if not impossible, task. One of the biggest obstacles they face is people who are resistant or defiant.

I always respond by bringing up the Diamond Principle. As a rule of thumb, the people in an organisation can be placed in three segments within a diamond: the top, the middle and the bottom.

The people at the top do not need much guidance or goading as they are typically self-motivated. The middle population constitutes the majority of any organisation. This is the group that requires most of your guidance towards positive change. Being the majority, their impact on the whole is significant. At the bottom of the diamond, there is a relatively small but vocal population of people who are the most resistant to change and very set in their ways. They require the most coaxing and cajoling.

The Diamond Principle reminds us not to use the bottom population to justify inaction with regard to positive change. When the bottom population is allowed to block change from taking place, we miss out on creating positive change for the middle and top populations, who constitute the majority in an organisation. We spend our time focusing on a minority who may not have the interests of the organisation at heart, instead of on people who would benefit a lot more from our time and guidance.

Do note, however, that we should do this without judging the minority in the bottom of the diamond. Remember that everyone in an organisation is fundamentally a human being, regardless of which segment they belong to.

Inquiry
1. Which segment am I focusing most of my energy and effort on?
2. Do I look at everyone in my team and organisations as fundamentally the same?

7

EQUAL VISION

Equal vision is the ability to look at things without any imagined or superimposed notions. One leadership activity that benefits greatly from the application of equal vision is the "distribution" of recognition and rewards to team members.

Consider a soccer team. In a soccer game, the goal-scorers are usually the ones who get all the limelight. We tend not to fully appreciate how the other team members contributed to getting the ball to the goal-scorer's foot. In the World Cup there is even a special prize for the top scorer (as well as goalkeeper and player). Likewise, in your team, are there also "top scorers" who get all the glory?

Being a leader requires us to be aware of such biases caused by tradition and practice. It is quite customary for sales teams to get the bulk of the attention because they bring in the money. But does that mean we overlook the contribution of the rest of the members in the organisation? To a mindful leader, everyone in the team is important. Think of equal vision as sunlight falling equally on all surfaces and objects.

In any large organisation, there are many "invisible" people we take for granted. We don't appreciate their value until something goes wrong, like the elevator breaking down or the washrooms not getting cleaned. This also applies to shared services and support departments who do not directly contribute to the top line. These groups of people are the unsung heroes of your team or organisation. Most of the time, they don't get their fair share of recognition.

In the same way, your leadership success is dependent on many people and factors. Try drawing a 360° diagram with yourself placed in the centre, surrounded by all the people and factors you can think of who have an influence on your success. The diagram will help you see that you are never solely responsible for your successes (or failures) – credit is also due to your team members, peers, external stakeholders, vendors, bosses, etc.

This does not mean that you need to distribute the fruits of your labour to others. Rather, it is a reminder that leadership success is part of a larger network of actions and reactions over which you have limited control.

If you extend this thinking to all your life's activities, you will realise that almost all of them are contributed to and caused by innumerable factors. You are not the absolute cause of every outcome in your life. So share the celebration with others, especially with those who may never get to be where you are.

Inquiry

1. Are there goal-scorers in my team who get more of my attention and resources?
2. Who are the people and teams that have contributed to my successes?

WEEK 2 MINDFULNESS PRACTICE

AWARENESS OF BREATH MEDITATION

Purpose

To learn to simply be with your breath and yourself without judgment. To be in a calm, non-judging awareness, allowing thoughts and feelings to come and go without getting caught up in them.

Method

- Find a comfortable seat which keeps your back upright and relaxed. Or have a seat on the ground.
- Sit comfortably; close your eyes if you like.
- Bring your attention to your breathing either by observing your nostrils or the rise and fall of your chest and abdomen.
- If thoughts distract you, simply notice those thoughts, then bring your attention back to your breathing.
- Bring curiosity to your practice. Is your breath fast or slow? Is it deep or shallow?
- It is natural for thoughts to enter into your awareness, and for your attention to follow them. No matter how many times this happens, just keep bringing your attention back to your breathing.
- As the meditation ends, give yourself credit for having spent this time in this state of being.

8

COMPASSION, EMPATHY AND KINDNESS

Compassion is perhaps the crowning glory of human beings. Other animals have been found to demonstrate compassion too, but it is only in human beings that it manifests in full measure.

The Bonobos ape, for example, spends much of its time being peaceful and not engaging in the sort of violence associated with other primates. They have also been found to show compassion and empathy – quite surprising for primates. This suggests to me that compassion and empathy are innate qualities.

In business culture, however, we seem to have forgotten about compassion, except when "compassionate leave" is given for a death in the family. But this is done as an act of policy rather than emanating from the leadership.

This is a pity, because compassion in a leader can be so powerful. It allows the leader's mind to be more sensitive to his team members' pain and difficulties with greater awareness. It allows team members to relate to the leader on a human level, and inspires them to reciprocate the compassion by doing their best to make sure their leaders do not fail. Compassion and empathy create a ripple effect.

While compassion is a "feeling" response, kindness is the "action" response. Kindness is the demonstration of compassion and concern. It may be extended not only when you see someone in pain, but also when a person is in need. Martin Seligman and Christopher Peterson have found kindness to be one of 24 character strengths that are universal across cultures and time. Leaders who are kind are always remembered and are very effective in keeping a team together.

Related to compassion and kindness is empathy. Empathy is the knowledge of another person's experience by looking at it from their perspective. In fact, empathy is what enables kindness, for without it you would not be able to know what another person is feeling. According to Daniel Goleman, "Empathy represents the foundation skill for all the social competencies important for work." Needless to say, the ability to empathise is a very important skill for leaders.

What I am saying here directly counters the ideal image of leaders as stoic, task-focused and hardy. In my view, compassion, empathy and kindness form a "triangle of humanity" for leadership. Without any one of these, a leader may be seen as autocratic or even bereft of humanity.

Recognise that you cannot make yourself become more compassionate, more empathic or kinder without first having compassion for yourself. Funnily, this can be harder than it sounds. I have seen people show a lot of kindness and compassion to other people and to animals but not to themselves. At times, forgiving a staff member is easier than forgiving yourself. Start with self-compassion and continue to look at yourself as a perpetual work-in-progress.

Inquiry

1. Who is someone in my team or organisation who is in difficulty or pain? What is the possible impact that this may have on the person?
2. What are the situations in my professional life where I have failed? Did I have compassion for myself?

9

COMPETING MINDFULLY

Competition is part and parcel of a capitalistic economy. Leaders have to ensure that competition does not put them or their organisation at a disadvantage – or out of business!

Kodak, a company with over 130 years of history, had to radically re-strategise in order to save itself from bankruptcy, while Nokia, once a giant of its industy, eventually had to sell off its mobile division to save itself. Only the fittest survive in the competitive global economy.

This ever-present threat of being out-run and made irrelevant is what drives competition and the whole business world. However, the flip side is that it also tends to create a sense of fear and insecurity among leaders.

Consider this example. There was a company A, which was owned by a large telco. A competitor telco, company B, wanted to place its mobile service antennae in A's property, so as to allow its customers to have reception while in A's premises. Visitors to A's premises had lodged numerous complaints to B citing bad reception. However, the request was turned down because A did not see why it should help a competitor. The visitors' experience and how that could impact decisions and business discussions at A's premises were not taken into account at all. This is a classic example of how A competed from a sense of fear and insecurity.

Is it possible to compete mindfully then? And how would that be done? The answer lies in competing not from a place of fear and insecurity but from a place of innovation and creativity.

THE 56-DAY LEADERSHIP JOURNEY

Take the example of 112-year-old company 3M, which has been very successful over a century due to one phenomenon: innovation. 3M placed unique structures, systems and values within its organisation that enabled the creation of revolutionary products such as Scotch tape and Post-it notes, to name a few. Through these efforts, 3M has remained competitive till today.

Innovation lies at the root of human behaviour and psychology. Our minds do not like boredom, and boredom sets in when we experience the same thing over and over again. We crave novel experiences. Mindfulness helps us understand the workings of our minds, so that we can align ourselves with it. Once we see that creativity and innovation are natural to the human mind, we can use that to spur competition in a mindful way.

There is a new-age view floating around that we should not compete at all. This view is rooted in the abundance mentality – the belief that there is no scarcity of resources, that there is enough for everyone for the indefinite future, and hence there is simply no need to compete. I have always been intrigued by this mentality because ontologically abundance does not exist. Abundance is like a unicorn that only exists as a figment of the imagination. For instance, we know for sure that the volume of oil and natural gas available in the world is finite and depleting fast. Holding on to an abundance mentality in the face of facts comes from the same place of fear and insecurity as does the scarcity mentality.

In summary, competition is natural, but how we compete differentiates the mindful leader from the rest. We should compete from the space of innovation and continue to notice the competitive instinct with non-judgment.

Inquiry

1. What new experiences have I enjoyed in my life? What made each of them novel?
2. What have been some of my most innovative moments? Study the environment and conditions of those moments.

10

EVERYTHING IS URGENT?

"Urgent" is a popular word in the workplace, to the point that it has become the norm. Clients have told me that they want a service delivered the very next day, or as soon as possible. I always wonder why it is that everything has become urgent these days. Perhaps it's because competition has become incredibly stiff, or our expectations are rising day by day.

Urgency is like a race against time. With the rapid changes taking place in the environment, customer preferences and our skills, time is of the essence. However, we must be mindful not to let urgency be the sole determinant of our actions. As Dwight D. Eisenhower once said:

> *I have two kinds of problems, the urgent and the important. The urgent are not important, and the important are never urgent.*

Be aware of where you are investing your mental energies. Are you focusing on the truly important things, or is your mind always racing against time to deliver services and products? Having too many urgent things on your plate can create stress, and also implies that the external environment has become uncontrollable.

It leaves you with no mind-space to focus on tasks that could be important.

I have noticed among many leaders an urgency to come to a decision or conclusion. In fact, leaders who make quick decisions seem to be well thought of by their team members. They like that a quick decision allows the team to take action as soon as possible and complete the task at hand. I have even heard people saying they like their bosses because they make decisions fast instead of asking for more time or delegating the decision-making power to the team member. As efficient as it may seem, I doubt the effectiveness of this approach.

Decisions do not have to be made quickly all the time. Different situations call for different approaches. While in urgent situations it is true that quick decision-making can be very useful, that's not the case with important matters. This is where mindfulness comes in. By delaying reaction, it hones our ability to be aware, attentive and accepting, to distinguish the urgent from the important, and to respond accordingly.

With mindfulness, we recognise that it is in the nature of the mind to want to converge on a solution as swiftly as possible. This translates to our placing similar expectations on the people we work with. Thus we may end up setting unrealistic targets and deadlines. But by making every task an urgent task, we distract our team members from what is important. This could possibly subject them to stress, anxiety and even burnout. A mindful leader is careful not to choose expedience over wholesomeness.

Inquiry

1. What are the emotions that I feel when my boss gives me an urgent task?

2. List down three urgent tasks and three important tasks at your job. What are the factors that make them either urgent or important? Were there any tasks that were both urgent and important?

11

CROSS-CULTURAL COMPETENCE

The world has become a global village in the last 50 years. Not only are we able to communicate across thousands of kilometres instantaneously, we are also moving across borders with greater ease. In 2015, 244 million people were found to be living in a country other than their country of birth.

I have witnessed this phenomenon in Singapore, where since the 1990s a large number of immigrants have come here to live and work and some have since made the country their home. Each year between 2012 and 2015, more than 1.2 million immigrants were in Singapore for work. The population of Singapore was about 5.6 million in 2017, which made one in every three people an immigrant. This phenomenon is not limited to Singapore – it is happening globally.

Today, the people you lead most likely come from a variety of cultural backgrounds. Or *you* may be the migrant, taking on a leadership role in a culture other than your own. Such situations can give rise to tension within the team due to different beliefs, cultural values, religious practices, languages, dietary habits, etc. Likewise, gender norms, expectations of power, individualism vs collectivism, etc., can significantly affect the beliefs, emotions and actions of team members.

I once met a seasoned executive coach who asked me incredulously if I ate with my bare hands. People of Indian descent – as well as people from the Middle East, Africa and the Malay archipelago – use their bare hands to eat (after washing them well, of course). This executive coach was shocked by the idea that people actually did this. She found the idea inconceivable, and further inquired if was it possible to tear meat with one's bare hands. She was genuinely curious!

As mindful leaders, the first thing we bring to such situations is non-judgment and acceptance. I remember walking into a meeting room once, where the usual business custom was to shake hands. I reached out my hand to greet the lady in the room, but instead of taking my hand, she pressed her palms together in greeting. I retracted my hand and reciprocated her greeting in the same way. A part of me was rather pleased that she was able to observe her culture without it affecting the business we intended to discuss. It goes to show that more often than not, diverse cultures can co-exist in harmony.

That said, we need to watch out for behaviour that crosses the line of cultural difference and begins to undermine the goals of the team or organisation. A mindful leader steps in to renegotiate and agree on working norms, doing so with objectivity and wholesomeness.

Inquiry
1. When noticing a practice or behaviour that is unknown to me, how can I best respond with curiosity and acceptance?
2. How can I create a working environment in which all cultures are seen as important?

12

VALUES

There are a few fundamental values that I consider very important for a leader. The first of these is truth. Truth is always a statement of fact. And facts create knowledge in the minds of listeners. Unless we see the connection between truth and knowledge, we may not see the value of truth and of expressing truth.

Sometimes the truth we need to communicate to our team members can be a hard one to take. In such situations, discretion is required. For example, organisations that are planning to downsize usually have to retrench some of their staff. Unfortunately, they tend to keep the news under wraps until the axe falls, leaving employees mired in anxiety, doubt and confusion.

Imagine if instead of this practice, organisations acted with truthfulness and transparency. There is a good chance that by engaging the whole organisation in sharing responsibility, we might inspire collective innovation and voluntary efforts to save the company. One of the best practices in downsizing, according to Kim Cameron of the Ross School of Business (University of Michigan), is to look at staff as assets and not to treat downsizing as a threat. This is consistent with the spirit of MIL – approaches such as this come from a place of truth-sharing and values.

Next comes a value that makes truth possible, and that is communication. A leader's ability to keep his team members informed is very important. The busyness of our work can sometimes make this a low priority, but just as the best marriages are built on non-judgment and respectful communication, likewise the integrity of a leader-member relationship depends very much on the same conditions.

The effect of this, over the long-term, is a deep level of trust between leaders and their team.

What if a leader's values are not aligned with those of his team members? This can create challenges. Most often, what happens is that the leader's values take precedence. Because of this, some members gradually lose their sense of belonging and ownership, because they feel their values are not considered important. Other team members may adopt the leader's values unthinkingly, eventually morphing into clones of the leader. In such situations, it is important to go back to the fundamental values of truth and transparency. Use these fundamentals as your basis for establishing the team's collective values.

Inquiry

1. What are the values of my team members? Have I asked this question to my team?
2. How open can I become with my team members? Can I communicate in a timely and truthful manner?

13

INADEQUACY

In mindfulness, the opposite of wholeness is the feeling of inadequacy. We are naturally disposed to feeling inadequate because we are always in a state of "need" with regard to health, wealth and knowledge. That is the nature of our body-sense-mind complex.

As children, we first experienced our inadequacy when our parents sent us to school because we needed knowledge. We went there to acquire knowledge. As we grew up, we felt inadequate socially because we did not have friends and thus went about forming a network of friends to give us support. In the workplace, we feel inadequate when we are unable to meet targets, which seem to get more unattainable each year.

In leadership, feelings of inadequacy can limit our effectiveness. We go through an inner battle with self-judgment, feeling ourselves incompetent or not good enough for our role. These thoughts lead to stress, anxiety and unhappiness. As a result, our performance is adversely affected.

The thing to remember about inadequacy, however, is that it only pertains to a specific domain. For example, I may be in need of negotiation skills – this makes me inadequate in that area, but in that area only. You cannot be inadequate *as a person*. So don't let any sense of inadequacy in a specific area become pervasive to the point where you feel small as a person.

The pervasiveness of our sense of inadequacy largely depends on how much value we have given to judgments about us by the external world as well as our self-judgment. When someone tells me that I am an irresponsible leader, it is actually a piece of information. But my inner sense of pervasive inadequacy quickly turns it into self-judgment, which creates self-talk statements such a "I am a useless manager" or "Nobody likes me in my team".

Leaders with a pervasive sense of inadequacy sometimes use their power to compensate for it. This makes their team members compliant, which gives the leaders a sense of adequacy in having control over others, which they equate with leadership.

For us to move away from such behaviour, self-awareness is required. This is where mindfulness comes in. It helps us to pierce through the smoke to see reality as it is, and to disassociate identities associated with self-judgments.

Inquiry

1. What are the areas of my leadership where I have noticed my limitations? Am I able to accept them?
2. What are the situations in which I have used my power and control to get things done?

14

HABITS AND ADDICTIONS

We are creatures of habit. Psychologists tell us that most of our habits form during childhood and continue to rule a big part of our behaviour, including our leadership behaviour. Say I was an unhappy child who threw a tantrum whenever faced with a problem, then as a leader I might demonstrate this same behaviour in work situations. I might get angry and lash out at others when things don't go my way. In short, we bring our childhood habits to work!

One specific habit that we can get locked into is addiction to success. This happens when we get so used to success and perfection that we cannot accept "falling short" or having to let go of a job title which once gave us power and status. This addiction to success can become pathological if not noticed and managed.

Early in my career, I knew a senior finance professional who committed suicide because he was laid off. It appeared that his suicide was not due to his loss of job, as might be expected, but the loss of identity. He had come to have an unhealthy reliance on his job to give him a sense of identity and achievement.

The addiction to success can be particularly disastrous for leaders, as researchers have found that people in senior management are more prone to addictive behaviours by virtue of their psychological traits – the same ones that took them to their leadership positions.

Noticing these tendencies in ourselves is an important aspect of MIL. A common blind spot is when we expect change from our team members in their addictions but not ourselves. Ask yourself if it is fair for you to expect change from others when you are not willing to recognise your own struggles with addiction. Such double standards do not help in being a leader who inspires performance.

Inquiry

1. What positive habits of mine have I brought from my childhood to my leadership?
2. What are the symptoms of my work addiction that I am aware of?

WEEK 3 MINDFULNESS PRACTICE

MINDFUL EATING

Purpose

This exercise involves paying pull attention to the experience of eating and drinking, both inside and outside the body.

Method

- Seeing: Look at your food. Take time to really focus on it with care and full attention. Look at it as if this is the first time you have seen it. Look at the presentation, plating, layout, colours, layers, smoothness and variety.
- Holding and touching: Take one spoonful or a piece of the food. What is the weight like? How does it feel? Is it smooth, rough or slimy? What else do you notice?
- Smelling: Bring the food closer to your nose. With each inhalation, take in the smell. Is it fragrant? Anything distinct about the smell? What memories, if any, does it trigger?
- Mouth: Place the food in your mouth, but don't start chewing yet. Notice how it gets into your mouth in the first place. Focus on the sensations and explore it with your tongue.
- Tasting: Take one bite into it and notice what happens. Notice the juice, flavour and sensations. Is it bitter, sweet, sour or salty? What is unique about the taste? Take another bite.
- Hearing: As you munch, notice the sound of chewing. What do you hear?
- Swallowing: Notice the sensations of swallowing.
- Take your next bite and chew as slowly as you can and explore the sensations in your mouth at your own pace.

15

TRUTH

The truth hurts, as the saying goes. As leaders, we need to know how to communicate truth effectively, especially when the recipient may not take favourably to hearing it.

In the tradition of mindfulness, three conditions are to be satisfied when speaking the truth:

1. Pleasing
2. Non-hurting
3. Beneficial

Pleasing – This refers to our choice of words when communicating the truth. The words we use have a direct impact on the receiver's mind. Negative words evoke emotions such as anger, sadness and hatred. They cause the listener to become defensive or hurt. On the other hand, using positive words when communicating the truth can evoke acceptance, enthusiasm and calmness.

Non-hurting – This refers to the intention of your communication of truth. Is your intention to hurt the listener? Hopefully not. But even if you don't mean to hurt, sometimes the receiver of the information may misinterpret your words and be hurt. So even with the best intentions, things are not entirely within your control; just try to pick your words carefully to minimise the chances of hurting others.

Beneficial – This means the truth should be beneficial to the listener. Sometimes, we want to point out something that is true, but it does not help the person to become better. Such communications should be avoided as they do not contribute to wholeness or wholesomeness.

Here is an example of a true statement communicated badly: "The project sponsor is unhappy with you. The project performance is bad and behind deadline."

Here is how it can be expressed better, in a manner that is pleasing, non-hurtful and beneficial: "The project has not met the critical milestones, although you have done your best. The project sponsor is unhappy about this. We need to get it back on track after understanding what has happened."

I once had a team member with a very positive personality who always welcomed feedback. One day, I needed to give him some unfavourable feedback, and I did so without considering the three conditions above. I felt that he was objective, wise and collected, but his response surprised me. He decided to quit the project. What this taught me is that even the most positive and objective of people will find hard truths very difficult to stomach. As leaders, we mustn't overestimate our team members' ability to receive truths objectively.

Inquiry

1. With whom can I communicate today or in the next few days to convey a difficult truth?
2. Are there people in my team who dislike truth? What can I do about it?

16

GRATITUDE

Gratitude is the emotion that arises when something meaningful is gifted to us. Other words associated with gratitude include thankfulness, appreciation, gift, meaningfulness and expression.

In leadership, we need to express our gratitude to our team members. Without them, we would not be where we are. In expressing your gratitude, tell them specifically what you are grateful for. Or else, they will never know if gratitude is the reason or if it is just a meaningless ritual to "show" that you are grateful.

I have always liked the cards on my gifts more than the gifts themselves. This is because the words in those cards can significantly change the way I look at the gifts. It is those words that I remember and am thankful for when I look at the things I have received from people. They give meaning to the gifts.

Today's discussions about meaning and happiness have tended to create a narcissism for only things that we like to do or things that align with our strengths. This is a very "walled up" understanding of meaning. It implies we are only grateful for things that go our way.

In mindfulness, we take a very broad view of meaning, We expand its limited boundaries to include both the things we like and things we dislike. We allow it to encompass all that has made us what we are, a combination of darkness and light, good and bad, right and wrong, likes and dislikes. We see everything that has happened in our lives as things that were meant to be. Gratitude pervades our being.

Inquiry

1. When was the last time I expressed my gratitude? What emotion did it create?
2. Think about a gift that you deemed to be worthless. What could be the intention of the giver?

17

FOCUS

One subset of paying attention is focusing (refer back to the Attention chapter). Focusing has two aspects. One is the practice of sustained noticing that is done during practices like awareness of breath, body scan and sitting meditation. The other is the choice we make at every moment to focus on certain things over others. We will discuss this latter sense of focusing in this insight.

More than ever, our lives are filled with distractions. Too many things around us compete for our attention, including our smartphones and other devices, As a result, we are finding it harder and harder to stay focused on a single task.

Back in 1995, Microsoft launched its Windows 95 operating system, and one of its selling points was "multi-tasking", i.e., the functionality of being able to open multiple applications at the same time, something that earlier operating systems did not offer. Multi-tasking was initially meant to describe the machines' functionality, but what happened was that human users started to imitate the behaviour, doing multiple things at once. Job advertisements and workplace literature began to regard multi-tasking as a generic job competency. I remember sitting in job interviews witnessing interviewers asking if the candidate could multi-task.

Today, researchers are telling us that multi-tasking is no good for our performance and unhealthy for our brains. In fact, it stresses and overloads the brain. The brain is at its best when it does one task with focus, i.e., mono-tasking. Mindfulness practices encourage us in the mono-tasking direction by bringing our focus to one thing at a time, such as through body scan and mindful eating.

In leadership, our biggest challenge is managing multiple members and teams, each with multiple tasks. This does not help our brains. Sometimes we are guilty of overloading our team members too, expecting them to complete tasks simultaneously. We should remember not to mistake the performance of multiple tasks with multi-tasking. The former is a reality at our jobs, but doing it all at the same time is multi-tasking, which leads to distracted thinking and poorer outcomes.

Inquiry

1. What are the current distractions at my work? Could there be a possibility of increasing mono-tasking?
2. What is something that has worked well in my leadership? Am I doing more of that?

18

HUMILITY

When I was a child, my Tamil teacher taught me these beautiful lines by the 13th-century poetess Avvai:

What you have learned is a mere handful;
What you have not learned is the size of the world.

Humility arises as a consequence of recognising one's imperfections and limitations. There are three significant facts of life that help us better appreciate humility. The first is our mortality, the second is power, the third is our limited knowledge. Let us talk about leadership mortality first.

Our leadership has an expiry date, just like everything else. Most of us are active at work for about 40 years of our lives; after that, we move into retirement. New leaders quickly take over our roles and we gradually fade into history. This fact of leadership mortality is inevitable, but it can be hard to accept, especially the more senior we get.

Secondly, our power is limited by the space we are in. The most powerful leadership role might be being president of a country, but even the president's power is limited; beyond his country, he has no direct power. Likewise in business, you may lead a team, department, division, line-of-business or the organisation – but your power is limited to your area of responsibility and goes no further.

Thirdly, it is impossible that we know everything in the world. As leaders, we depend on subject matter experts and our team members to contribute to our knowledge. Only as a team can we increase our knowledge multifold.

The limits of time, power and knowledge show us that we are not as big as we think we are. They are reasons for us to be humble. There is always someone who is more powerful, more knowledgeable or with a better track record. There is always a time and space boundary beyond which our leadership holds no sway.

The opposite of humility is narcissism – an exaggerated regard for one's abilities and accomplishments. Studies have shown that narcissistic leaders are also as successful. However, such leaders do not give enough attention to the means to the end. Narcissism makes heroes out of zeroes. Humility treads the middle path between zero and hero.

The "strengths movement" can also sometimes create an exaggerated notion of oneself. This movement calls for radically replacing the focus on weaknesses with a focus on strengths. It gives the false idea that you will gain more by improving your strengths rather than working on your weaknesses. While this may be true in exceptional situations, it is a balanced perspective that works.

I liken a leader to a potter, who uses what is already on the potting wheel to create something valuable and beautiful, which was not there in the lump of clay. The more we recognise that we cannot create anything new in this world and that all we do is to manipulate what is already there, the more humble we become. That is all we are doing. The sum total of the energy in the universe is constant. You can only work with what you have at your disposal.

Inquiry
1. How many times has my role changed in my career? How long have I been a leader?
2. Give some thought to your leadership mortality. What are the emotions that arise along with these reflections?

19

ABUNDANCE AND SCARCITY MINDSETS

Zebras are abundant in the wild. They are easy prey for lions, tigers, cheetahs, hyenas and crocodiles. The predators do not compete for the zebras as there are more than enough of them. This is how we view abundance. The abundance mentality assumes that there are plenty of resources to go around – like the zebras – and that we can share the available resources like the predators do.

The scarcity or deficit mentality, on the other hand, is when we assume that we are always lacking in resources even though we may be adequate. It is also a very prevalent mindset. Even as we move from being a developing nation to a developed one, people still do not lose this deficit mentality. The deficit mentality is the opposite of the abundance mentality. Neither one is desirable.

The primary concern I have with the two mindsets is that they do not reveal the actual nature of things. The abundance mindset creates an illusion of security and fantasy which do not exist, and promotes a sense of individualism as opposed to collectivism. For example, an oil and gas company continues to drill excessively because they "believe" that there is enough to go around. And people continue to overpopulate the Earth despite the limited resources available today.

The scarcity mindset, for its part, operates on the premise that there is not enough to go around, and hence we need to acquire as much as we can, before anyone else does!

The strange thing, then, is that both mindsets, despite coming from opposing beliefs, encourage competition and exploitation.

One of the important topics taken up in mindfulness traditions is the study of ontology and epistemology. Ontology is concerned with the "existence of things and what they are", while epistemology is concerned with "how we know these things".

With mindfulness, we see that we do not need to subscribe to either of these mindsets to be successful. We learn to look at things as they are, without any projections. As leaders, we need to recognise the pitfalls of the two mindsets as they betray all material evidence and at most create motivation in the minds of the needy.

Inquiry
1. What are the resources available in abundance in the world?
2. What are the resources that are depleting in this world? What could I do as a leader to decelerate its depletion?

20

YOU ARE NOT THE ROLE

First and foremost, leadership is a role; it is not you. You are larger than the role. In our lives, we play many roles, such as being a son, mother, brother, citizen, resident, employee, etc. Each role is unique, but some roles may overlap. Each role is played in different situations. When you enter your office you are a manager, and when you return home you are a mother. At a particular stage of your life, you were a student and then at some point you let go of that role, and picked up a new role.

None of the roles we play in life are absolute or permanent. They rise in time and they expire in time. Some have longer life-spans and some have shorter ones. But they are always finite.

Sometimes you may play two or more roles at the same time. For example, in coaching your staff for performance, you take on the roles of both manager and coach. Situations like this may give rise to a conflict between the roles. As a coach, you are expected to be neutral and help people succeed. But as a manager, you cannot be neutral – your team member's success is as good as yours. This can lead to a sense of distrust among your team. A mindful leader needs to recognise the possibility of such conflicts.

Almost all roles are dependent on a host of other factors or people. Your role as a citizen depends on the country. The role of a son is performed with reference to his parents. A leader depends on his team. Without members to lead, a leader is not born.

The roles we play all have a distinct purpose and require unique competencies. Leadership has a clear purpose, as identified by your organisation based on its goals. The competencies required are also based on what is necessary to achieve the set goals. The purpose, goals and competencies of the role may vary from time to time.

When roles change, purpose and competencies change too. This happens when you are promoted or redeployed, or when you switch jobs. It is therefore important to take stock of what is required for the new role.

When roles change, new perspectives emerge. I have seen that happening with my friends who lived a carefree life in their single years. After marriage, their lifestyle and values changed. And when they became parents, all of a sudden their children's well-being became of paramount importance to them. Similarly, as leaders, our members' well-being should be of paramount importance apart from business goals.

All your roles depend on *you* for their existence. Without you, these roles have no real value or meaning. They depend on you for their existence the way a wave depends on water. The *you* I am referring to is the *being* that you are. Your being is bigger than any of these roles that come and go. These roles arise in your being while your being does not depend on them. When your leadership role undergoes stress, misery, failure, success or admiration, your being does not get affected by it. It is the role that is impacted, not you. Your wholeness of being is the sum total of all of the roles and its experiences in the present moment. Your whole being beholds all of these roles.

Inquiry

1. List down the roles that you are currently playing. Rank them based on the value you attribute to each of them. What does that tell you?
2. Identify the roles that make you happy and then the roles that cause you stress or unhappiness. Do you see any patterns?

21

HAPPINESS

Earlier on in the book (in the Attention chapter), I talked about the purpose of life being happiness. Leaders need to recognise that people may be inclined to one of the two paths to happiness, namely hedonia and eudaimonia. In this insight, I am going to take you further down the slippery path of happiness.

As a leader, whose happiness is the most important to you: your own, your team's, your boss's, or your investors'? Whose happiness would you sacrifice first in a difficult situation? These are very important and difficult questions as most often leaders attempt to keep either their bosses or their team members happy, and when they fail, they completely ditch the idea of making anyone happy.

Leaders who take the path of keeping everyone happy may find it a difficult task because happiness gets very complicated when it comes to others. When push comes to shove, leaders most often end up sacrificing the happiness of their members first – because it is the easiest thing to do. They make sure to keep their bosses happy, though. But what about your customers? You, your boss and your team would very well agree that your customers need to be happy for your organisation to be successful. In the end, everyone in the company is unhappy trying to keep your customers happy. Is this not an irony?

Well, if we can't please everyone, should we at least expect our jobs to make *us* happy? This is another common pitfall. The expectation that your job needs to make you happy is as good as the expectation that your train rides, your children, your education, the weather and everything else should make you happy. All this does is set you up for failure – because you did not sign up for this job or take up the reins of leadership for happiness. I believe that if your job makes you happy, it is a bonus.

Finally, research tells us that happy employees tend to perform better than those who are miserable. A mindful leader allows his team members to discover what makes them happy, the same way he is on a journey of discovery. While mindfulness by itself may not be able create that happiness, it allows us to be aware of the universality of happiness as the purpose of life.

Inquiry

1. What are the things that make my team members happy, apart from monetary rewards?
2. What path of happiness am I on: hedonia or eudaimonia?

WEEK 4 MINDFULNESS PRACTICE

SITTING MEDITATION

Purpose
To be with yourself and to look within. This is an opportunity for you to be in a state of *being* as opposed to be in a state of *doing*.

Method
- Find a comfortable seat which keeps your back upright and relaxed.
- As you get comfortable in your seat, bring your attention to your breathing.
- Do not manipulate or change your breath in any way. Simply be aware of it.
- Observe the breath deep down in your belly. Feel the abdomen as it expands gently on the in-breath, and as it falls back on the out-breath.
- Every time you find your mind wandering away from your breath, gently bring it back.
- Now as you observe your breathing, you may find from time to time that you are becoming aware of sensations in your body. Just notice them with curiosity.
- As you maintain awareness of your breathing, expand the awareness to feel your body, from head to toe, and become aware of all the sensations.
- Expand your awareness to include thoughts as they move through your mind.
- As the meditation ends, give yourself credit for having spent this time in this state of being.

22

THOUGHTS ARE THOUGHTS, NOT YOU

The nature of thoughts is perhaps one of the most interesting subjects in mindfulness. While it may not directly influence your leadership, it is sure to help you better understand your mind.

The first fact about thoughts is that you do not have absolute control over them. By control I am referring to the ability to create, sustain and stop a thought. If we had control, then we would not get angry, jealous or sad. There would be no need for psychotherapists or mental health professionals. The fact that we have these professions tells us much about our mind and thoughts.

Thoughts rising in succession is the second fact. Every thought rises on the basis of a prior thought. For example, you see your CEO in the lift lobby. The next thought in your head is about having to deliver a report to him by this weekend. And then the next thought is about the party you need to prepare for during the weekend. Perception triggers a thought and then more thoughts are triggered in succession. All our thoughts have their root in either perception or memory. They have a life of their own. They may come when you least expect them and then leave on their own accord.

The third fact is that we cannot predict our thoughts. Try predicting what thought you will have in five minutes' time. Even the best psychologist can't do this. We appear to be ruled by our thoughts because they just simply happen, without our permission or approval.

Most thoughts fall into the categories of information, emotion and action. Thoughts can be information when our sensory organs report data. For example: This is sweet, loud, hot, bright, etc. Emotions are another form of thought. An emotion's valence (refer back to the Awareness chapter) depends on whether you like or dislike the object or experience. For example, if a rose is something you love, you would experience positive emotions upon seeing one. If roses remind you of a broken relationship, however, you would experience sadness. Finally, thoughts can also be about action, which is the motivation to do something about the triggering perception.

The interesting thing about our mind is that we own certain types of thoughts and try to disown others. We cherish thoughts that we like and that are favourable. We ruminate on them. As for thoughts we dislike, we try to reject them, but in the process end up "auto-ruminating" on them. It is like telling you not to think of an apple, which results in the apple appearing in your mind. In mindfulness we practise acceptance – by accepting our thoughts, they gradually vanish on their own.

The final and most important fact I would like to share is that you are not your thoughts. Instead, you are *aware of* your thoughts. Thoughts rise in you like waves in water. Unless and until you take ownership of these thoughts, they do not have the power to overpower you. That is the reason why an ill-action done to you by a stranger does not have as much of an impact as when the same action is done to you by a loved one.

Your sense of wholeness includes all of your thoughts and not just a select range of thoughts. This is how acceptance can be developed. This significantly helps you as a person and as a leader. It reduces the transference of stress, pressure, sorrow and a host of other emotions.

Inquiry
1. Where do thoughts come from?
2. Can thoughts define my being?

23
DEALING WITH CHANGE

Change is a big challenge in organisations and leadership. As the maxim goes, "Change is the only constant". The challenge for leaders with regard to change is not how to implement change but understanding the very nature of change.

Change can be seen as positive or negative depending on who benefits and who loses. It is usually the organisation that benefits from planned change, while staff are adversely affected. The leaders may see the need for change, but they are often unable to make the rest of the members of the organisation see it too.

The mindfulness perspective of change is that it is natural. There is nothing in this world that does not undergo change. It is the very nature of every object to change. This is the objective view of change. Yet our minds are very much attached to the changelessness of things because change implies many things, from the need to put in effort to adapt as well as to keep things as they are. Babies cry the moment they see a new face because of the unfamiliarity. The comfort and security that changelessness provides is sometimes irresistible. Therefore, resistance to change is quite natural to our minds.

A mindful leader recognises that his team members' resistance to change is natural and does not warrant judgment. What is needed is the ability to implement change in a manner that appeals to the way the human mind works. People are accepting of change when they can control it or be involved in it. Instead of being steamrolled by change, team members can be encouraged to be in the driver's seat, to be change agents themselves.

I would personally recommend the Appreciative Inquiry process for introducing change as it appeals to the human mind by providing higher engagement. Through this process, leaders involve their whole team or organisation in effecting positive change, by identifying and appreciating what is working well and then doing more of it.

That being so, the fact is that even when we are not allowed to be part of the change process, our minds learn to adapt to it eventually. This forced adaptation is itself natural to the human mind. That is how the human civilisation has survived natural calamities, plagues, wars, revolutions. The only drawback of such adaptation in organisations is that it stifles performance and sustainability. It is better for leaders to deal with change mindfully rather than passively.

In many parts of the world, people buy caged birds in order to set them free. Most of these birds, born and bred in captivity, are unable to survive in the new environment they are released into. What appeared to be a positive change for the bird turns out to be a potentially fatal problem. Instead, if we were really interested in improving the bird's well-being, perhaps we should avoid such drastic change, and think how to improve the existing environment. Perhaps the bird could be housed in a bigger cage, or placed in an aviary.

This principle applies to us humans as well. Drastic change and sudden freedom can destabilise. Change is better when it is gradual. It is good to be in the grey before proceeding to being white.

Our eyes teach us a great lesson everyday. When you wake up in the morning in your darkened bedroom, your eyes have time to adjust to the bright light of day. If you woke up to bright light immediately, your eyes would find that torturous.

In mindfulness, your *"being"* witnesses change taking place, detached from the change, merely observing it. This helps a lot in viewing change as an object in your awareness rather than identifying with change itself. You neither become swept away by the force of change, or put up a futile effort to resist it. Like watching a film projected on a movie screen, you witness the projection of change on your screen of awareness.

Inquiry

1. What are the change efforts I have been part of in my career? What did I notice?
2. Is change something my mind welcomes or something it wishes did not happen?

24

RESPECT

I was once leading an important project across the border from Singapore. I needed something fixed, and gave firm instructions to one of the workers employed by a contractor there to get it done within seven days. To my dismay, the job was not done even after 14 days. When I asked why, the contractor did not even bother to explain.

Later on, I was told by the supervising staff at the overseas office that the way to influence people in their culture was to treat them with respect. So I approached the worker again, this time talking to him in a more respectful and requesting manner, rather than giving him orders. The task was completed within the next hour.

Respect is crucial in leadership. There is a big difference between demanding respect and earning respect. In regimental systems, respect and obedience are very much part of programmed behaviour. Any senior officer is to be respected by a salute. While this behaviour is perhaps traditional and important in the defence forces, in civilian society leaders have to earn their respect.

Respect can be earned as an outcome of inspiration. I have had respect for the bosses in my life not out of demand but inspiration. Their decisions, values and actions inspired me to respect them. It was not even a conscious choice but a natural response of one human being to another.

An interesting thing about respect I have found is that it's easier to respect people we do not know than those we do. Distance engenders admiration while close proximity reveals the "dust and dirt". As we become more familiar with a person, our level of respect often fades. This is because our minds are always searching for that perfect, ideal person. The less we know about a person, the more we are able to imagine them as perfect; once we know more, our mind starts to judge. Remember that in reality the perfect person does not exist. Don't let an illusory ideal affect how you regard and treat others.

As leaders, we may sometimes be tempted to put down people outside our immediate team or organisation, in an attempt to boost morale, for example. I have noticed some leaders' habit of disrespecting or speaking ill of stakeholders or competitors to their team members. In fact I have done the same, too, in the past.

Being mindful means that we give respect to everyone without judgment. If we believe that our team members deserve greater respect than the members of another department or the workers employed by the contractors, we have got it all wrong. Everyone deserves our respect as a human being. Even criminals on death row deserve respect, for while their actions may have led them to this fate, we do not need to punish them a second time around.

In Mindfulness-Informed Leadership, respect is lodged in our hearts when we relate to people regardless of their social status, political position or seniority. We earn our respect by respecting others.

Inquiry

1. Do I expect my team members to respect me because I am a leader? Why?
2. Is there a difference in the way I speak to and treat my team members, my bosses and strangers?

25

TRANSPARENCY

Transparency is another key factor that makes leadership more effective. Being transparent means that as a leader, you reveal your values, intentions, goals, likes and dislikes, emotions, etc., truthfully, to the people who matter.

First and foremost, transparency evokes authenticity in leadership. Team members get to see who their leader is and understand you better. Trying to put up a facade is definitely not being transparent. I know some leaders who are hard on the outside but soft on the inside, or vice versa. This is neither authentic nor transparent. We

THE 56-DAY LEADERSHIP JOURNEY

should be ourselves as much as possible. Putting up a facade is the reason why some people are good personally but not professionally – they appear to project two selves.

Being transparent also creates trust, so that your team members do not misjudge you and your intentions. Very often, when we make decisions, we do not explain our considerations for making that decision. Instead we use the excuse that it was decided in the board room, so that we can avoid having to go into the reasons, which may be complicated. However, when people are left in the dark, unable to see through the "opaque" wall of your response, a sense of distrust starts to grow.

Does transparency mean you have to share everything in your life with everybody? This is not the case. Not every detail about you needs to be made known to the world. People only need to know about you insofar as the information is relevant in a particular situation.

In fact, over-sharing has its problems. I have encountered people who share everything about themselves, to the point that it creates distrust. This could be possible because our lives are not like islands. We relate with many people in our lives, and over-sharing inevitably reveals possibly intimate details about their values, behaviours and lives to others. These people have taken us into their confidence; indiscriminate sharing suggests that we are indiscreet or have ulterior motives.

So rather than be an "open book", use discretion in your self-disclosure. It is only valuable if you use it in the right time, place and circumstance. Or else it may backfire.

Inquiry

1. What are the emotions that I am comfortable sharing with my team members?
2. What are the limits of my self-disclosure as a leader?

26

AUTONOMY, POWER AND CONTROL

The small man builds cages for everyone.
— Hafiz

In the past, leaders tended to hold all the power, whether at the national level or in business. Today, in developed countries, power appears to be more distributed, and likewise in the workplace. With global literacy rates doubling in the last hundred years, we are seeing more educated and empowered young people entering the workforce. Traditional perceptions of power and control may not work with these generations who started their lives with autonomy. Leadership today is not about power but about the distribution of power.

But won't ceding power to others make leaders redundant? This brings us to the question of our need for control. I have seen experienced leaders and managers who love to control the thinking and behaviour of their members. The need for control stems from insecurity and the fear of failure. It becomes convenient for leaders to take that path of total control because it assures them of expected results.

Some leaders go even further and try to create a deep dependency on themselves, so that they remain valuable and relevant in the organisation. The damage is that members never learn from their experiences, and as leaders we are burdened with great mental baggage.

If instead we learnt to empower our team members, we would free up our own mental resources, to contribute to the progress of the organisation. Empowering others demonstrates our ability to build trust, explore acceptance and nurture relationships with people. It also means that we are not afraid to fail and willing to learn from it. A mindful leader does not seek to be in total control because that implies he thinks he knows it all – which is quite the opposite of being humble.

I remember a time when I was leading a project sponsored by a senior leader. During one of the weekly project updates, I tried to shift the responsibility of making a decision to him. Instead he asked for my recommendation, which caught me off-guard. This completely shifted the responsibility of justification onto my shoulders. It allowed me to expand my horizons and see my proposed recommendation – which would cost an additional 10% over budget – from different perspectives. I had an opportunity to use wholesomeness as a vision for my justifications. In the end, my recommendation was accepted and implemented. This incident showed me that empowerment can enable wholesome thinking in the minds of leaders. And it would not have happened if the senior leader had not let go of his need for control.

I have seen so many organisations where the permission-and-approval culture is prevalent. Team members don't feel empowered to make decisions, and don't take ownership of the work they do. They end up with the attitude of simply ticking the boxes, preferring to be merely compliant rather than innovative. Such organisations will not be able to soar, because the bar is set.

Being a mindful leader would then mean that we pay attention to psychological phenomena such as power, control, autonomy, empowerment and freedom, and understand the intimate connection they have with our team or our organisation's ability to continually raise the bar.

Inquiry

1. How do I get people to do things that I want done? How do I influence?
2. To what level and degree are my team members free to make decisions and justify them?

27

PERFORMANCE AND MEASUREMENT

Managing the performance of our teams is an important function of leaders. Almost all medium and large organisations have a formal performance management system in place for doing this. One-on-ones are also used as an informal way to assess performance.

What I am specifically interested in here is how we handle those team members of ours whose performance is below expectations.

The first thing that I have noticed is a tendency for leaders to scold or admonish underperforming staff. In a workshop that I was facilitating, one manager asked if being angry and acting from anger was okay. I asked him if his organisation paid him a salary to be angry or to do his job well. Was there any part of his job description that said he was entitled to get angry, be disappointed or to have any other emotion? As funny as it sounds, we sometimes do feel that it is perfectly fine to get angry and scold our team members.

Anger and scolding may get you obedience, yes, but it also creates a climate of fear within your team. By angrily scolding an underperforming team member, you turn the issue from an objective one into a personal one, and stray away from organisational objectives.

The Broaden-and-Build theory, developed by Barbara Fredrickson in 1988, gives us additional insight into how to deliver performance feedback in a wholesome way. One of the interesting discoveries of this theory was the 3:1 ratio. It was found that every time we give negative feedback to a team member, it takes three instances of positive feedback to restore the person.

The other thing our mind has is an "instinct" to punish. We tend to want to penalise people who do not perform up to expectations, in the belief that it will get them to improve. But in fact, this is not a natural instinct at all. Compassion and kindness are the mind's very nature. The drive to punish and penalise comes from the "eye for an eye" basis of our justice system, which we take as sacrosanct, but which is not suitable for human relationships as its aims are retributive rather than rehabilitative. Punishment runs counter to the human purpose of happiness and success.

Mindfulness helps in making a positive shift by allowing us to develop compassion and kindness. The loving kindness meditation is a practice that specifically develops these traits.

Inquiry

1. What are my thoughts, feelings and behaviours when I see low performance among my team members?
2. What are the possible emotions in the minds of my team members when I give feedback?

28

SOLITUDE AND REST

Being alone can reveal to us a great deal about the nature of our minds. I recommend the practice of disconnecting from sensory engagements and being alone for about 30 minutes to an hour once a month or even weekly. This provides a good opportunity for a retreat into your inner space.

Or try and find some time for solitude in the course of your work day, even if it's just five to ten minutes once a week. Sometimes, I take the opportunity to lunch alone and thereafter sit in a garden spot for about ten minutes. These short sessions allow my mind to prime itself and even find solutions that would otherwise be unknown to me during my busy engagements at work.

Devices have become too much of a distraction these days, preventing us from being mindful and focused. It would be wise to keep your devices away during your time in solitude. These "unplugged" moments with yourself are priceless. They allow the busy mind to rest and look within.

Regular, spaced-out practices are better than toiling hard for 11 months of the year then taking a month-long vacation to rest it off. Such an approach creates a dichotomy between rest and work. In mindfulness, we do not specially create an opportunity to be mindful but are mindful in every opportunity we have.

I also do not recommend silent retreats that stretch beyond a day because this goes against human nature and creates the same dichotomy. We are social creatures, hence mindfulness and solitude have to be integrated into our lives rather than being an *event*. True, the first formal steps you take into the world of mindfulness will be formal "events", but as you go along, mindfulness will slowly glide into a way of being.

Finally, do not underestimate the value of good sleep. Sleep rests the mind and helps you to stay focused during the day. Research has shown that sleeping less than seven hours reduces well-being. To be mindful leader, you need to be at your rested best.

Inquiry

1. What are the personal devices that I carry along with me? How much time do I devote to using these devices every day?
2. What do I do to disrupt natural silence around me? What does my behaviour tell me about the value I accord to silence?

WEEK 5 MINDFULNESS PRACTICE

MINDFUL WALKING

Purpose

- Mindfulness is not about just stillness. Being mindful in walking integrates mindfulness into daily life.
- Mindful walking is not about arriving at your destination or rushing to finish your walk, but simply being mindful that you are walking and that you are breathing. We arrive with every step.

Method

- Begin your walk by acknowledging that you are beginning it.
- Walk with your eyes fixed on the ground about a few steps out.
- Feel the sensation in each foot as it presses down onto the earth or floor.
- Notice your foot as it lifts up, touches the ground and is lifted up again. Follow the movement and the feeling of each footstep with your mind and your breath.
- Notice which part of your foot leaves the ground at the end of each step.
- Notice which part strikes the ground first at the beginning of each step.
- Try walking faster for a few seconds and notice the difference in how your feet feel.
- Slow down to a slow walk. Notice the difference in your heartbeat and body sensations.
- Gradually slow to a stop. Notice the sensations in your feet once you have come to a complete stop.

29

LOCUS OF CONTROL

Locus of control refers to the level of influence one has over situations and events. People with an external locus of control tend to attribute events in their life to external factors and other people. On the other hand, people with an internal locus of control tend to believe that they have full control over results and situations in their life.

Leaders with an external locus of control may exhibit a couple of tendencies, foremost among which is blaming others. I have encountered leaders who totally divest themselves of responsibility for issues that make them look bad. They blame their team members as well as external parties for the problems and failures. By doing that, the mind immunises itself from all that is unfavourable and that which does not benefit the individual. This contributes to a blame culture in teams and organisations.

On the flip side, when they do succeed, such leaders tend to identify others as the cause of success. They may not claim ownership of successes as well. So it cuts both ways, although the blame culture is perhaps more unwholesome.

The blame culture is also related to a fault-finding tendency found in most of us. Leaders with a strong external locus of control are often more critical and judgmental of others. I used to have this tendency and as someone trained as an engineer it served me well. I am naturally very inclined to troubleshoot or find the root cause of equipment failures in my job. It is a strength for engineers to be able to do that. However, as leaders we are not dealing with machines, but people. This tendency also extends to seeing the bottle as half-empty most of the time instead of half-full, creating stress on our team members.

On the other hand, leaders with a strong internal locus of control tend to blame themselves for everything and take responsibility for all success and failures. The failures that get owned up to by such leaders also contribute to stress.

While people do have a dispositional preference for either the external locus of control or the internal, more often it is situational and value-based. What most of us do reactively is to own all that is successful and blame others for the failures. However, this is detrimental to leadership as it unconsciously promotes the very culture in the team or organisation itself. As a result, cohesion is eroded and eventually performance is stifled.

Mindfulness helps us in noticing our locus of control when faced with both favourable and unfavourable situations. We then look at both successes and failures as outcomes of collective effort. This promotes the celebration of successes together and sharing the pain of failures together. Mindfulness practices enable an objective view of things and the recognition that results do not have a single cause.

Inquiry
1. Do I have a disposition towards an internal or external locus of control?
2. How does that impact my behaviour as a leader?

30

CURIOSITY AND KNOWLEDGE

Curiosity is one of the key attitudes of mindfulness. It creates impetus for new knowledge, and leads to deeper insights about oneself when adopted in mindfulness practices. With curiosity we can start noticing our thoughts, emotions and actions.

On the other hand, curiosity also killed the cat. It can create an incessant need for knowledge. Unregulated curiosity results in a barrage of information that does not get transformed into learning. One must be able to evaluate and synthesise the information to do justice to one's curiosity.

This is called higher-order thinking in Bloom's Taxonomy, a learning model that represents learning as taking place through six cognitive processes. Knowledge is only properly assimilated when it is processed through these six steps.

1. Remembering – The ability to recall knowledge from memory
2. Understanding – Making meaning of what is known
3. Applying – Using the knowledge
4. Analysing – Breaking down the knowledge gained into discrete functions
5. Evaluating – Making judgments and critiquing
6. Creating (Synthesis) – Putting all the processed elements together to form a harmonious and coherent whole

One key function of learning is applying knowledge. This applies to mindfulness as well – hence this 56-day journey, which allows you to go through the six-step process to arrive at Creating.

For a leader, it is important that information is not acquired for the sake of information alone. Too much information creates a bottle-neck and stifles the creation of the whole. If information does not get integrated into your very being, it becomes unhealthy and leads to confusion. It is like sharpening an axe day after day but never using it or even checking if it works.

I have observed a tendency in many people to keep reading and exposing oneself to new information without ever integrating it. The mind takes on whatever is read, but instead of applying it, it continues to acquire new pieces of information. The new informa-tion replaces the old information, and the information to come will replace the current information. It goes on like a chain.

This impacts two important areas. Firstly, it prevents us from per-forming because we have not crossed the experimentation stage (applying and analysing). Secondly, our team members do not know who we are as we keep changing as we experiment.

Mindfulness keeps us in check by bringing awareness to the infor-mation we gather in our minds and helping us not to overload it. An important question to ask ourselves when faced with a piece of information is whether it serves the purpose of our leadership.

Inquiry
1. Which stage of Bloom's Taxonomy am I at right now with Mind-fulness-Informed Leadership?
2. What do I need to be aware of with regard to information gath-ering and knowledge?

31

PERSPECTIVES

Three blind men come across a baby elephant. One touches the elephant's leg and says that it is a tree trunk. Another man touches the elephant's trunk and calls out that it is a snake. The third man touches the elephant's body and says it is a sack of grains. Yes, let us discuss perspectives. All of the three perspectives could be taken as true or you could equally view them all as false.

In one country, a commuter train breakdown might be a national issue; in another country, a national issue might be landmines. I was travelling in the Himalayan ranges more than 15 years ago and I saw this kid who was probably four years old. She was walking around the snowy ranges in her bare feet and a thin dress, while I was dressed in three layers of clothing. The same environment but different responses.

Two drivers meet at a bar. One earns US$250,000 a year and transports 500 people a day. The second driver earns US$54,000 a year and transports 1,250 people a day. The former is a pilot and the latter a train driver.

The two countries with the largest economies in the world are China and the USA. One is socialist and the other a democracy.

A friend of mine is a vegetarian because he hates animals so much that can't imagine having them in his stomach. Another vegetarian I met told me that as a kid he disliked the taste of meat and eggs and hence decided to go vegan. You can choose to become vegetarian because you love animals or because you hate them or for some other reason.

Even freedom can be interpreted differently. For some, freedom means the freedom of speech; for others, it means freedom from the tyranny of corrupt politicians.

The word "good", too, can be very subjective as it does not tell us anything. Good for whom, and why and what is so good about it? Two different things can be considered good. Two people can consider the same thing to be good and bad.

People also define happiness differently in different cultures. In a study spanning 182 countries, it was found that while happiness is what everyone seeks, what exactly makes people happy varies dramatically. For example, Americans associate happiness with high arousal emotions while Hongkongers associate happiness with neutral emotional states such as relaxation and tranquillity.

Leaders and team members may have different perspectives. One side isn't better than the other. Nor is one right and the other wrong. Yet sometimes one appears to be more right than the other. Maybe one is more relevant in a given time, place or circumstance, but it is not absolutely more valuable than the other. Believing that your perspective is correct or superior in absolute terms is as good as considering the trunk of the elephant to be a snake.

Inquiry
1. Are perspectives true or false?
2. How easy or hard is it for me to accept a view that is different from mine?

32

THE "WHY" QUESTION

In the Six Sigma system, which was developed to improve manufacturing processes, practitioners ask a series of five "why" questions as a way to uncover the root cause of any given defect. On the contrary, coaches and psychotherapists abhor "why" questions. Interesting, isn't it? One way to explain this divergence is that coaches and psychotherapists do not consider human beings as defects to be analysed but as works-in-progress.

Compare these two pairs of questions:

1. Why did you go there? *vs* What got you there?
2. Why are you late? *vs* You are late. What happened?

In each pair, the first question has a tinge of judgment embedded in it, as if the questioner wants to judge you based on your values, decisions and beliefs. It feels intrusive, like an interrogation. Asking your team members "why" can make them feel like they are facing a firing squad.

In MIL, we are more interested in the "what" questions followed by the "hows". These questions shed light on objective data. Asking "why" can baffle people because we do not always know the "whys" of things! It is the "what" and "how" that are clearer to us – we are better at describing what we know about a situation or problem than explaining how they came to be.

That said, "why" questions do not have to be avoided completely. They can be useful when you ask them of yourself. This helps to uncover your intentions as well as your assumptions. So, as a principle, use the "whys" on yourself and the "whats" and "hows" with your team members.

Inquiry
1. What is my intention when I ask "why" questions?
2. Is the root cause important when a team member approaches me with a problem? Why?

33

DOING VS BEING

We are usually in a state of *doing*. Doing one thing or another constantly has become the norm. A busy person is constantly doing something, be it answering emails, running from meeting room to meeting room, having lots of conversations, or attending to his devices constantly. Being busy can become a habit for some of us.

What do we even understand by "doing"? Some seem to think that running on a jogging track, for example, is considered "doing" but resting in a chair is not. This is a misunderstanding we have with respect to doing. The sense of doing is a kind of compulsion to "do" something to accomplish a goal or purpose.

The sense of *being*, on the other hand, is about having awareness, paying attention and practising acceptance while engaging in activities. It is about being present in all the activities of "doing". It is about noticing all that is happening internally and externally, naturally and non-judgmentally. This state of being is actually the very nature of awareness or self-awareness.

Hence, it is not a case of doing vs being. Some discourses try and present doing and being as mutually exclusive, but that's not how our minds and bodies work. We cannot stay away from performing actions as our physical make-up is meant for it. But yet we are called human beings – rather than "human doings" – for a reason. We are "beings" capable of paying attention to the present experience and being aware of it. And it is out of this being that arises doing, which becomes a natural response in awareness.

As leaders, it is important that we are not in the state of doing all the time. We should cultivate, through mindfulness practices, the ability to *be* while doing. This is what will make our sense of doing a product of wisdom.

Inquiry
1. How can I describe my being in my own words?
2. How would I know if I am anchored in my being while doing?

34

TRUST

Trust is one of the building blocks of relationships – in business and in personal life. Marriage, friendship, business partnerships and leadership all require a strong foundation of trust in order to flourish.

Trust is built both ways, meaning that we need to trust others for others to trust us. There are five ways in which we can develop trust, which are embedded in the word itself:

T – Truth
R – Reliability
U – Understanding
S – Sincerity
T – Transparency

Firstly, we need to value truth. The value of truth has already been discussed (refer to Day 15) – team members trust a leader who values truth and speaks the truth. To maintain this trust, a mindful leader speaks the truth always with the intention of bringing out the best in the listener.

Reliability and trust have perhaps the strongest relationship. Reliability relates to consistency and predictability in behaviour over time. A good leader responds to situations in a consistent way and does not make exceptions without providing a rationale. Over time, your team members not only get to know you better, they also feel that they can rely on you to help them when things go wrong or are about to go wrong. A reliable leader is like a safety net that team members trust will save them from a bad fall.

Leaders who take the time to understand their team members will build trust with them. Those who don't tend to be perceived as know-it-alls or lacking in empathy. An understanding leader also makes it a point to see situations from his team members' perspective.

Sincerity is defined as being genuine and honest. Telling people that they are on the right path when they are not or keeping quiet when things are not heading in the right direction is the opposite of sincerity. I have had encounters with people whom I trusted that fell short of this expectation. Leaders need to be sincere even when dealing with difficult truths.

Finally, transparency and openness are also required in building trust – which we discussed in Day 25's insight.

Mindfulness practices help us to recognise the trust that is required in our leadership as well as in our team members. When trust is built, hope dawns. Hope reflects optimism and only an optimistic culture can survive through storms and upheavals to transform into greatness.

Inquiry
1. How can I be aware of TRUST in my leadership?
2. Who is a person I trust? How have they have demonstrated TRUST?

35

LIKES AND DISLIKES

One of the most popular discourses in the business world today is choosing a profession we *like*. I have encountered many advocates of this school of thought in the last decade or so. However, the discussion about doing only what you like to do can get a little complicated.

Studies show that the hedonic value of our actions has a great positive impact on our performance. People who love art tend to create astounding art pieces. People who love research become great researchers, while people who love marketing become great marketers.

Although such examples may be true, the principle of choosing to do what you like assumes that there are abundant opportunities for jobs that you love doing. As we all know, however, resources are limited, and there is quite a high chance that what you like doing may not be available or achievable in a given space, time and circumstance. So it may not be possible for everyone to do what they like best.

Furthermore, there is the underlying assumption that what we like is always right and what we dislike is always wrong. An extreme example of this would be a leader like Adolf Hitler or Idi Amin who committed atrocities while enjoying it. I am pretty sure these leaders loved what they were doing, having political control over a country and its people. They did all that was contrary to the values of humanity and yet many people followed them. This a classic illustration that people who like what they do may not be right after all. This can apply to your life as a leader too, because your inclination towards what you like may not be what is wholesome for your team, department or organisation.

Conversely, what you dislike may be the right thing to do in a given situation. For example, as a manager I used to submit my quarterly profit-and-loss reports to the Chief Financial Officer. I disliked doing this as it was a tedious and time-consuming exercise in scrutinising numbers. However, it was in the best interests of the organisation as the reports were crucial "pulse checks" as to how the company was faring in terms of its finances.

To make things even more complex, likes and dislikes also change over time. We may like something today, but not tomorrow, or in another place or in another circumstance.

I have often found that some team members become very good at pleasing their leaders when they know what the leaders like and dislike. While there is some strategic value in this approach, it can end up reinforcing the leaders' biases. I once worked with an organisation where the middle management only told the top management what they wanted to hear. They painted a rosy picture of affairs regardless of what was happening in reality, because the top management did not like to hear about things that had gone wrong. Things did not end well for that organisation.

A mindful leader does not identify with his likes and dislikes, or insist on their superiority and timelessness. Rather, in mindfulness we constantly recognise the arbitrary nature of leading and living with likes and dislikes.

Inquiry

1. Are effective leaders always well liked by their members?
2. What would be the impact if my team members knew my likes and dislikes?

WEEK 6 MINDFULNESS PRACTICE

THREE-MINUTE COPING BREATHING SPACE

Purpose

This exercise helps you step out of "autopilot" mode and bring yourself into the awareness of the present moment. It is especially valuable when your thoughts are moving in a negative direction.

Method

1. AWARENESS
   - Adopt a comfortable standing posture, keeping your body relaxed.
   - Become aware of your body and the surface on which you are standing.
   - Then ask yourself:
   - What is my experience right now in my thoughts?
   - Acknowledge thoughts as mental events.
   - What am I feeling?
   - What are some bodily sensations?
   - Acknowledge and accept your experience.

2. BREATHING
   - Gently redirect your full attention to breathing.
   - Notice the belly rising and falling with every breath.

3. CONSCIOUS EXPANSION
   - Expand the field of your awareness around your breathing.
   - Include the sense of the body as a whole, your posture, and facial expression.

36

COMFORT

As leaders, we have to get used to being comfortable doing the uncomfortable. Comfort is linked to what we like, familiarity and our habits – therefore, being comfortable is not necessarily a good thing for leaders of teams and organisations.

The pitfall of comfort is that it assumes that things will always remain the same. But it is in the nature of things to change. Hence, it behoves us to be always receptive to doing the uncomfortable.

We are usually at our best when things go as we expected. But when things go south, we get unsettled. The test of leadership is not when times are great but when the going gets tough. That is when we recognise the nature of our mind, values and wisdom. Comfort and discomfort can be great teachers.

When we are comfortable for too long, it could be a sign that the environment is stagnating – or we are stagnating – and radical change will soon take place. Leaders of companies that have been successful over a length of time tend to review their strategy periodically. We should similarly take stock of our comforts and discomforts regularly, and adjust ourselves accordingly.

Inquiry
1. How do I behave in uncomfortable situations?
2. What are the things that make me uncomfortable?

37

OBJECTIVITY VS SUBJECTIVITY

One key mental ability that gets developed as an outcome of mindfulness practices is objectivity. Objectivity is a sense of impartiality and the absence of biases. The opposite of objectivity is subjectivity, which is influenced by our feelings, tastes and opinions.

While we all know that objectivity is what creates a fair and just world, we also realise that it is quite impossible for us to completely stay away from being subjective.

In fact, subjectivity is not a dirty word at all. The world of art, for example, thrives on subjectivity. It allows us to look at things in diverse ways with sensual appreciation. It accentuates our emotional experiences and makes us human.

In leadership, too much subjectivity can sometimes hamper our effectiveness by making us hard to predict or understand. On the other hand, too much objectivity is also not healthy, as it can make us too logical and appear bereft of emotions. A mindful leader therefore needs to find a balance between objectivity and subjectivity.

One of the big challenges of subjectivity in leadership is the presence of biases. Biases prevent us from being objective and potentially lead to misunderstanding and unhappiness among our team members. Here are a couple of cognitive biases that plague leadership:

- Confirmation Bias – Making conclusions about a situation first and thereafter looking for evidence to support it.

- Curse of Knowledge Bias – Knowing a lot more than other people about a topic and therefore finding it very difficult to understand what others see.
- Empathy Gap Bias – Not being aware that your emotions and feelings have influenced your decisions or thinking. This applies to your team members as well.
- Outcome Bias – Judging the outcome and completely disregarding the decision made.
- Stereotype Bias – Labelling groups of people with characteristics without real evidence. This can severely impact performance evaluation as well as hiring.
- Authority Bias – This is when your members feel that you are right simply because you have authority.
- Egocentric Bias – Relying too heavily on your own perspective and having a disproportionately high opinion of yourself. An example of this bias is when you claim credit for a success when in fact your team members were the ones who were responsible for it.
- Halo Effect – Assuming that a person's positive attributes in one area are also present in another area.
- Self-Serving Bias – Interpreting events in a way that benefits yourself. This can also be selective hearing and only seeing what you want to see.
- Recency Effect – The tendency to remember only recent events and allowing that to influence the outcome for a long sequence of events.
- Same-Like-Me Bias – Being attracted to people who are similar to you.

Inquiry

1. What are the biases that I am more prone to?
2. How can I bring more balance to subjectivity and objectivity in my leadership?

38

THE ONE SOLUTION

A single solution that can fix all problems does not exist. The sooner we recognise this fact, the better we can be living our lives.

In mindfulness we learn to accept facts as they are. In fact, the function of knowledge is to present a piece of information as it is without altering the object. One of the philosophical definitions of mindfulness is the "constant recollection of the nature of realities".

This brings us to the way we perceive problems in our lives and in organisations. We often look for a single solution that can fix all problems in one shot. This belief in finding that one solution can sometimes create a sense of fanaticism and polarisation. History informs us that wars and conflicts were often directly or indirectly caused by this assumption that "I have found a solution".

This applies to organisations as well, when we assume that a single intervention can be a cure-all. Service providers, too, sing the same tune. A carpenter believes that all solutions are made of wood; a blacksmith believes that all solutions are made of metal.

But the problems of the world are far too complex to have a single solution to fix all its problems. We should instead recognise organisations and individuals as complex beings with multiple parts making up the whole. Each part has specific needs and hence requires a unique solution.

Whether these multiple solutions lead to a desired goal depends on time, experience, knowledge, people and a host of other factors. It is like a fishing net, where tugging one end may affect or unsettle other parts of the net. Every part of the net is interconnected.

Hence, being mindful means that we face challenges and problems with the awareness that individuals and organisations are diverse and complex, and a single solution will not do the job. We are also mindful that a solution of today could become a problem of tomorrow.

A reporter once asked me if mindfulness guarantees results. To his surprise, I responded with a firm "No". I explained that mindfulness is not a panacea; it works only under "favourable conditions". If you believe that you have found answers through this daily insight, please read it again.

Inquiry

1. Are solutions bound by time, place and circumstances?
2. Have I ever encountered a solution that has stood unchanged over time?

39

BELIEFS

Our brains have an innate tendency to believe in things. Beliefs help us to overcome our negative emotions and induce positive emotions. I am not referring to religious beliefs as they operate on the premise of a different epistemological framework. I am specifically referring to our beliefs about things and people that help us cope with challenges and assure us of stability. Sometimes these beliefs can also be influenced by our worldview and our religious subscriptions.

What we are interested in here is the way beliefs work on our minds and how they impact our lives and leadership. Beliefs can influence our emotions and behaviour, and alter the way we see the world.

For example, if we subscribed to the belief that people are bad, we would automatically assume that our team members are bad and that their motivations are bad too. We would naturally interpret their actions as malicious, especially if the outcomes are unfavourable. Distrust would be the norm.

On the other hand, if we believed that people are good, then we would use that to excuse our team members for doing something wrong. There is a certain naiveté that comes along with such behaviour.

However, beliefs are not facts. Facts are knowledge while beliefs are not. Both of the statements above – people are bad, people are good – are not facts because they generalise a group and force us to apply that belief on every person we meet.

What's more, beliefs give rise to different emotions. The belief that people are bad evokes fear, insecurity, distrust, disgust, etc. The belief that people are good evokes happiness, joy, wonder, excitement. Sometimes we choose to subscribe to a belief that gives us only the positive emotions. Thereafter we decide on an action that stems from the emotions triggered.

As leaders, we should be noticing all of these tendencies and the nature of beliefs and its impact on leadership. The awareness of our beliefs is very important as they severely impact our emotions and actions. While it is impossible to neutralise all our beliefs from our minds, the first step is to notice and accept them.

Inquiry

1. What are my cherished beliefs and how do they influence my leadership?
2. Do I tend to flock together with members and colleagues who share the same beliefs as me?

40

POSITIVITY AND STRENGTHS

In a conversation with a senior leader, I was told of an interesting incident. During the annual performance appraisal exercise, she encountered a strange appraisal by one of her managers. The appraisal form had two sections, one for recording the strengths of the appraisee and the other where the appraiser wrote about areas of improvement. To her dismay she found that only the section on areas of improvement was filled – for all seven members of the manager's team! She enquired with the manager if something went wrong, and in response the manager shared that he could not find any strengths in his team members.

Strengths spotting is a very important skill for leaders, but it can sometimes be difficult, as our minds are used to homing in on areas for improvement before anything else. It requires awareness to spot strengths in people. Everyone has strengths in some area. If you dig deep, you can probably even find some strengths in the most heinous of persons. As the proverb goes, "Even a broken clock is right twice a day".

Mindfulness practices help in developing a focus on strengths, positivity, and an appreciative mindset. They steer us away from looking for deficits and weaknesses in people. That doesn't mean we should be blind to weaknesses, however. Your areas of weakness could be a "derailer" for your career and for your team members too.

Therefore, a mindful leader works on both weaknesses and strengths. Fixating on strengths is like insisting a glass is half full; fixating on weaknesses is like insisting it is half empty. In mindfulness, we neither see the bottle as half-empty nor as half-full. We just see a glass of water. And as we notice that, the mind naturally learns to be positive without having to do it deliberately. Only then can wisdom arise.

Inquiry

1. What are the strengths I have noticed in my team members?
2. How can I help in further leveraging their strengths?

41

IDEALISM AND OPTIMISM

Idealism combines an overly optimistic and hyper-cheerful state of mind with the belief in a utopian state in which everything is perfect. Such thinking is often wrongly associated with mindfulness and meditative disciplines or contemplative philosophies. This mistaken assumption may arise because idealistic people also tend to possess a high internal locus of control or are sometimes highly eudaimonic.

Some business professionals have this vision that their organisation can be converted into a utopia where every staff member is happy every second of the day. This "ideal" state goes against the fundamental premises of mindfulness. It pushes the mind to polarise itself towards hedonia. It leaves us perpetually wanting and seeking, forever unable to accept the present state.

Idealistic thinking isn't a big problem if we view it as a private reality or the pursuit of someone who lives apart from society. However, in a world where we interact with others all the time, it comes up hard against objective reality. In objectivity we co-create and share truths as well as negotiate it in collaboration.

Idealism can also be turned inwards, when we construct an ideal self. This, too, goes against what mindfulness teaches us: not to superimpose our imagined realities on anything, including ourselves.

Idealism is not the same as optimism or positivity. Optimism is important because it can motivate us to fill the half glass of water to fullness; there is nevertheless a limit to how much you need to make it full. On the other hand, idealism imagines something bigger than what the glass is.

Being optimistic is also quite different from having an optimism bias, which is to believe that things will be better in the future. The opposite of this phenomenon is the pessimism bias, where people believe that negative things will happen to them. Both of these biases are rooted in non-acceptance. I have had some acquaintances who always assured me that "Tomorrow will be better" or that my business in the future would be exceedingly successful, but all that did was to burden my mind by asking it to surrender to some unknowable force.

Optimism, on the other hand, lies not in leaving things to an unknown force but rather having the locus of knowledge or action in oneself.

Hence, as leaders we need to be aware about idealistic thinking as well as its related biases.

Inquiry

1. Is it possible to be cheerful in a situation where we have failed or when our members have failed?
2. Is optimism important in leading people? Why?

42

LUCK

One of the least discussed topics in business is luck. Luck tends to be a dirty word in both business and leadership because it shifts the burden of responsibility to an unknown force, and we do not like the thought that we are not in control.

During my years of leading projects from idea to realisation, I worked with multiple suppliers and contractors who competed to win projects. What I learnt was that there is no one fixed formula for success. There are always so many variables, from submitting a reasonable price, to explaining the proposal convincingly, to providing adequate information; and very importantly, there are many factors not within a team's control. These include environmental factors, affordability, the state of mind of the approver, the team leader's unconscious biases, etc.

This led me to define luck as a series of unpredictable, unfathomable and sophisticated causes and effects. Luck is the reason why two people selling the same product at the same time and price may get different results. When your action or self-effort aligns with time, place and circumstances to produce favourable outcomes, we call it luck.

Action may not be able to guarantee luck, but there is no luck without action. Marketing guru Guy Kawasaki has said that working hard increases your chances of being lucky: "I'd rather be lucky than smart. It's funny though, that the people who work the hardest seem the luckiest, too."

Since luck is beyond our control, how should we respond when "bad luck" seems to dog us?

> *Emphasising what's in your control allows you to*
> *adopt an attitude of equanimity toward luck. You've*
> *done what you can, and from there you have to live*
> *with the results – good or bad.*
> — Michael Mauboussin

And that is the reason why acceptance and response are so important for leaders. There are times when you are not lucky and times when you are. It is not that you have gotten it right or wrong. Apart from your action, a series of unpredictable, unfathomable and sophisticated factors has also contributed to the result. Be aware of the nature of luck, and respond – not react – appropriately.

Inquiry
1. Have I had experiences where hard work and intelligence did not produce the desired results?
2. How would I deal with my team's stroke of unfathomable failures?

WEEK 7 MINDFULNESS PRACTICE

MINDFUL MOVEMENT

Purpose

To bring awareness to movement and to explore the different insights that may arise through movement.

Method

- While seated or standing, gently bring awareness to your body.
- Do a quick scan of your body from your feet to the top of your head.
- Notice any movements and bring your awareness to those movements.
- Raise your left arm slowly to the sky and notice the sensations as you move it. Gently lower it while noticing the sensations. Repeat the action with your right arm.
- Raise both your arms to the sky and notice the sensations. Slowly bring lower them and notice the difference in the blood flow and any other sensations.
- Slowly move your hips to the left and the right and notice the sensations of the movement.
- Raise your left foot off the floor as high as you can and notice the movements and sensations. Repeat with your right foot.
- Do a slow stretch of your whole body and notice the sensations.

43

WHOLENESS

My goal is not so much to be good,
as much as it is to be whole.
— Alanis Morissette

The subject of wholeness occupies a central place in mindfulness traditions. Wholeness can be seen from two important perspectives: one refers to your whole being, which includes both your bright and dark sides; the other refers to the wholeness of your innate awareness, present at all times and during all activities.

Being whole means that we accept what we are by noticing what we have within ourselves without judgment. It is not about neglecting the weaknesses and challenges that we have. It is about recognising them and even being comfortable talking about them objectively.

Positivity advocates often find it difficult to accept negativity and as a result become highly judgmental. Such thinking does not contribute to wholeness. As Todd Kashdan and Robert Biswas-Diener put it:

There is a not-so-hidden prejudice against negative
states, and the consequence of avoiding these states
is that you inadvertently stunt your growth, maturity,
adventure, and meaning and purpose in life.

By accepting all that we are, we develop a certain degree of maturity and resilience. We are not lesser beings anymore. I have encountered people who struggle to handle their thoughts and to find a way out of situations and environments. Wholeness is about noticing your irritations, your emotional triggers and even your own self-defeating thoughts.

It is truly great when a leader can see his team members as whole beings, and is capable of recognising their wholeness and developing them from their wholeness. To do so, leaders need to discover wholeness within themselves too.

The second perspective of wholeness is the very state of awareness. It is experienced in all mindfulness practices as we drop our judgments and practise acceptance. Your presence and being do not depend on what you *have* but what you *are.* It is not your goodness that makes you whole or the lack of it that makes you lesser. In the present state, you are indeed whole, and this becomes clearer to your mind in the moments when you drop all judgments.

This attitude allows your leadership to come from a place of neutrality, which is especially important when you need to make executive decisions. The greatest leaders bring out the best in themselves and others not as a wilful act but from their state of being, as a natural response arising out of their awareness, acceptance and attention.

Inquiry
1. What are the negative and positive emotions that I frequently experience?
2. How would I enable the vision of wholeness in my team members?

44

EQUALITY

The striving to make the world equal is an interesting discussion that has taken centrestage in many philosophies from time immemorial. There are various philosophies that propound the virtues of having an equal vision towards all. These ideas of equality touch our hearts.

But in practice, is true equality achievable?

Economic and political theories such a Marxism, Communism and Socialism appear to be aimed at removing the barriers of inequality but instead ended up creating another kind of class system. The caste system has also been severely criticised but we have just replaced it with a different class system, in the form of autocracy, democracy and aristocracy.

It seems that while all of us desire an equal world, we do not want to lose our privilege and our access to comforts and resources. It feels so natural that the world is made up of "haves" and "have-nots". And we subconsciously feel that some people are more "deserving" than others..

I have seen, for example, leaders who make it a point never to keep their CEO or senior leaders waiting for a meeting, but who would not hesitate to keep their staff waiting on them. Staff working at VIP lounges never get to be VIPs. People who sell luxury designer products never get to use them even once in their life.

Another thing that is happening is labour exploitation. People work in conditions where they have limited freedom. I have encountered companies that hire workers from third-world countries paying them one-third of the local salary and housing them in crowded dormitories. Many domestic workers around the world are not allowed to use their mobile phones during work and some of them have to ask permission before they can have their meals. Low-cost labour from one perspective is as good as slavery.

To be sure, absolute equality is not possible in this world. It is a law of nature that the universe can only function when it is not in equilibrium, for then we would have stasis and stagnation. What is needed in society and organisations is a social equilibrium to counteract extreme inequality. As leaders, we need to constantly do our part to maintain this healthy social equilibrium through the way we treat people.

I remember a cold night in January 2007 in Philadelphia, when I was having dinner in a restaurant with my friends. There was a small commotion at one of the other tables, and I saw that the waiters were trying remove a homeless lady from the restaurant. She was seeking warmth inside the restaurant on that freezing cold night. I had never witnessed such a scene in my life before, and it really broke my heart.

I wish that as mindful leaders we can do something to reduce the pain in this world. It starts right in our backyard. There are many things within our influence and power that we can do to reduce inequality, especially when it comes to human pain and suffering.

Mindfulness helps us to recognise that we are all fundamentally human beings. All ideas of social status, economic status and achievements are for functional needs. Beneath the garb of status and success, all of us wish for a great day each morning. And all of us universally use toilets regardless of who we are.

While equality is not possible, equity – which is what is needed for a healthy social equilibrium – is possible and it has to be one of the goals of mindful leadership. The desire for an equal world narrows the gap.

Inquiry

1. Can there be a sense of inequality even when leaders treat everyone equally?
2. Have I witnessed acts of exploitation? What were my thoughts during the incident?

45

BIG-PICTURE THINKING

With mindfulness practices, the ability to look at the big picture of one's business or organisation – which is a very important trait for leaders – gets enhanced.

I liken an organisation to the human body. What the mouth consumes affects every part of the body. What the brain does by processing information and makes decisions helps the whole body. Our limbs allow us to move and to transact. Everything that is done by our organs has a value and all the organs have a unified purpose. And that is what leaders do: unify the organisation towards a common purpose.

The absence of a big-picture perspective in a leader leads to internal conflict and eventual system failure. Thus, a mindful leader reinforces the inter-dependence and inter-connectedness of life as it is in business.

A larger consequence of such thinking is the leader's ability to see the organisation as part of society, as part of the world. I like Body Shop's mission to promote social activism, help people in third-world countries, and lead environmental campaigns; all of this is done without displacing business objectives and without the organisation being a charity.

Today, there is an increasing number of social businesses and social enterprises around the globe. That is the kind of leadership that I call mindful, where we pay attention to what is happening around us as well as within us, and thereafter take action.

Big-picture thinking also means not choosing what you want to see. Some of us have this mindset that the business unit is more important than the support units like the finance department, human resources, facilities, etc. This mindset gives undue importance to a select few people or units within a business and opposes the vision of the organisation being an organism.

Sometimes, the body needs special attention. For example, a medical diagnosis tells you that your calcium levels are low. This would call for an appropriate response, such as a change in diet. Taking too much calcium, however, could cause other problems. A measured, holistic approach is needed.

Similarly, a big-picture perspective helps leaders balance the needs of all parts of their organisation. At times we may need to focus on specific areas that require extra nourishment, but we are careful not to do so at the expense of the whole. Better still, we are able to see which other parts of the organisation can be enlisted to help heal the ailing body part.

Mindful leadership inspires co-creation and co-operation among people to solve problems with a bigger picture in mind. This is what Klaus Schwab calls contextual intelligence for leaders, which allows you to see the big picture and connect the dots. This helps in anticipating what is to come in the world of business, which is constantly changing.

Inquiry

1. Have I witnessed territorial instincts in other leaders who wanted to protect their turf? What are my thoughts about it?
2. How can I model big-picture thinking in my leadership?

46

SILENCE

The quieter you become, the more you can hear.
— Ram Dass

More than 10 years ago, I spent some time in the Himalayan ranges. One day, while out walking with my friends, we came across a monk in a small cave, with a group of people seated in front of him. We approached, and the seated people beckoned us to join them. As we got closer, the monk gave us a wide smile in invitation. Happily, we sat down with the rest of the group, hoping to listen to the monk's teachings. For a long time we sat there, but he did not speak. It got a little weird so we asked those seated what was going on. They told us that the monk was upholding a vow of silence that he had taken some two years ago. This man had not spoken in two years! Can you believe that? And then, the next question that came to my mind was: Why were these people seated in front of him if he wasn't talking?

This incident taught me a great lesson. One can have followers or listeners regardless of whether you speak or not. If you speak wisely, people may find you attractive; if you are silent, people could find that a teaching too.

While I am not entirely sure if another person's silence can teach you very much, I am very certain that your *own* silence can teach you a great deal.

Silence on the personal level is the absence of verbal activity. This state allows you to focus on and pay attention to your thoughts. Almost all of the formal mindfulness practices are observed in silence. It is good to practise silence daily, even it's for just two minutes, and avoid using any device or being in the "doing" mode during this time. In fact, this is more useful than going for a silent retreat for several days. It is within our daily transactions that we need to find time for silence.

One of the opportunities for this in our leadership is to create deliberate silence before the start of a meeting or discussion. Even spending some time in silence before a one-on-one chat can be immensely helpful in priming our minds.

However, silence is not golden when a response is required. For example, remaining silent when someone asks you a question is definitely not a mindful practice, and neither is the passive silence when you witness others doing things that are unacceptable.

> *The world suffers a lot. Not because of the violence of bad people. But because of the silence of the good people.*
> — Napoléon Bonaparte

Inquiry

1. What are the opportunities I have to create deliberate silence?
2. How do I respond to the silence of my team members during meetings and conversations?

47

TIME

Let's talk about time. Time is a reality that is invisible. It is not something tangible like this book. It is not like any other thing because in reality it does not exist anywhere except in our minds. The 12-hour clock that we invented and agree to follow universally is purely arbitrary.

What we do when we measure time is to measure change. In elementary physics, we are taught to measure change between t1 and t2. Unless something changes, time cannot be measured. Hence, time is actually change. Every time you look at your watch, you are witnessing change – the change of the Earth's position relative to the sun.

In mindfulness we notice change in time non-judgmentally. This reduces the impact of relative time. This attitude has a significant impact on leadership because all results and performance are measured in time. When we regard time as the yardstick for performance, it gives us the illusion that we cannot control it. But change is surely within our sphere of influence.

Through mindfulness practices, we bring our awareness to the change that is happening behind a task, and we realise that we are able to manage time through change.

I have noticed that between the time we identify a task and the performance of the task, many things may change. Without understanding this aspect of change, we can never move to a state of action. For example, your team members' success in accomplishing a task depends on many mutable factors, both internal and external. If you don't pay sufficient attention to these details, you may dehumanise the relationship that you are nurturing with your team.

By focusing on time, we are task-oriented, but by paying attention to change, we recognise the reality of life and humanise our relations with others.

Inquiry

1. How can I manage the tasks of my team with a change focus as well as a time focus?
2. Can tasks be handled in a more people-centred way rather than task-centred?

48

GENDER

One of the 17 goals set by the United Nations for transforming the world is gender equality. Women are not universally respected in all parts of the world. Although womanhood is generally respected in all cultures, this does not always translate to respect towards women individually.

Women are often seen as the caregiver, moral exemplar, child-bearer, mother and wife. These roles are not salaried. Men have greater access to education and go on to work and bring in the income. These images have been set in the minds of many men as well as women. Having said that, I am pretty sure that most of us do not discriminate against women consciously; what I am concerned about here is unconscious discrimination.

I was once co-interviewing a female candidate for a job opening. The conversation went well and I was impressed by her social and emotional awareness. All of a sudden, my male co-interviewer asked if she was planning to get married, to which she answered yes. He then asked if she was planning to have a child soon. I was shocked by these questions and immediately steered the interview back towards her competencies.

In another incident, a female colleague of mine in a different team learned that she was pregnant after several years of trying. Her gynaecologist encouraged her to take a three-month break from work to rest as she found her womb to be weak. When she shared the news with the senior leader of her department, he was very happy for her, and agreed that she should take the three months off. He approached the Human Capital Management department to put up this request. Their response was that it was possible, but she would not be guaranteed of the job when she returned.

The question I have for leaders is: Do you think about policies first or do you think about what is best for your people and the organisation?

Without eulogising the role of motherhood, I see womanhood as just another role, like manhood. They are not the same, but they are both important in different spheres of our life. Today's ideas about leadership usually come from men. From an internet search on the top ten leadership gurus, it looks like most of them are men. I'm sure you are not surprised by this fact. And I'm also sure that you will not be surprised to know that more men are in prison than women.

As mindful leaders of today and tomorrow, we also have to look out for the needs of the "third gender", as well as the lesbian, gay, bisexual, transsexual and queer (LGBTQ) community. People who identify with these groups are human beings above all else and experience the same emotions as you and I do. Sexual orientation and identity shouldn't make a difference to how you treat your team members and how you value them. Awareness does not have a gender.

Inquiry

1. What are my views on gender differences and on creating a positive world for all genders?
2. As a leader, how can I work with all genders without judgment and prejudice?

49

CONSUMPTION VS CONTRIBUTION

During one of my regular runs at the park near my home, I saw two families with young children playing by the river. The parents of one family were teaching their kids how to fish with a net. The other family was engrossed in feeding the fish and turtles. This incident gave me an insight on the phenomena of consumption and contribution. One family was consuming and the other was contributing.

In our leadership, do we contribute more or consume more? A consumer could be someone who looks forward to earning his salary, accolades and rewards. A contributing leader, on the other hand, gives value to his team and organisation by his wisdom.

As human beings, we tend to consume more than we contribute. The challenges this creates for our minds are diverse. One result is the lack of altruism and volunteerism in societies globally. Another is exploitation. When we have a consumption mentality, we seek to *use* the people and resources at our disposal. This idea of using a person or a thing can potentially lead to exploitation. A mindful leader does not use, but *utilises*, leveraging the strengths of people and resources to create value.

Our infatuation with novelty is one major reason why we consume more than we need. Novelty induces the release of dopamine in our brains and this becomes an addiction or sorts.

This can even lead to excessive mental consumption. I know of people who study too much. As virtuous as it may sound, learning can become mentally binding if there is no contribution. We may end up living in an idealistic world completely divorced from pragmatism due to the lack of contribution from what we have learned.

On the other end of the spectrum, there are people who pay it forward and do not expect any reward, whether now or in the here-after. I once met an Uber driver who had been a very successful sales director of a multi-national FMCG company. He shared with me that from time to time he travelled to Thailand to contribute money towards the education of poor Thai children. I asked if he felt rewarded when he did these acts of charity. "I never give to receive," he replied. "I give without expecting any kind of reward."

This is the spirit of contribution. Having consumed, we act by contributing. This creates a symbiotic relationship between the roles of consumer and contributor. Warren Buffett is a fine example of someone who while being one of the richest men in the world has devoted a lot of his time to philanthropy. He does not give and give, but gives as well as takes. This is a key principle in life as well as in leadership.

As leaders we need to pay attention to our consumption and balance it with our contributions. This awareness starts early, like the children at the river.

Inquiry

1. How much am I consuming and contributing as a leader?
2. What would I consider my most valuable contribution to the world?

WEEK 8 MINDFULNESS PRACTICE

LOVING KINDNESS MEDITATION

Purpose

To expand kindness through cultivating heartfulness and increasing self-love.

Method

In this meditation, allow yourself to switch from the usual mode of doing to a mode of being. At the same time, be aware of the movement of your breath, the in-breath and the out-breath.

A. Bring to mind someone for whom you have deep feelings of love. Notice your feelings for them arise in your body. Whatever the effects, allow them to be felt. Now let go of this person in your mind, and see if you can offer loving kindness to yourself, by letting these words become your words mentally:

May I be well

May I be happy

May I be healthy

May I be free from suffering

Notice the feelings that arise and let them be.

B. When you are comfortable, try offering loving kindness to someone who supports you, who has always been "on your side". Bring this person to mind, imagine them perhaps across from you, and let these words become your words mentally:

May you be well

May you be happy

May you be healthy

May you be free from suffering

C. Once your feelings flow easily to a loved one, turn your attention now to someone you have difficulty with – it is best not to start with the most difficult person, but perhaps someone who brings up feelings of irritation or annoyance. See if you can let these words become your words mentally as you keep this person in your awareness:

May you be well

May you be happy

May you be healthy

May you be free from suffering

Notice the sensations and feelings that arise within you. And see if you can just let them be.

D. Bring to mind the broader community you are a part of. You might imagine your family, your workmates, your staff, your neighbours, or indeed all the people and creatures on the planet. Include yourself in this offering of loving kindness, as you let these words become your words mentally:

May all be well

May all be happy

May all be healthy

May all be free from suffering

May all overcome their obstacles

May all see goodness

May all attain their cherished desires

May all be happy always

Notice the sensations and feelings that arise within you. Sit with them for a few moments until you are ready to end the practice with the following words:

May I be able to forgive all living beings

May they always be able to forgive me

May there be friendship amongst all living beings

May I have no hatred of anyone

50

SEEING WHAT YOU WANT TO SEE

What do you see in the image below?

Do you see a young lady or an old woman? You'll either see one or the other – our minds are not able to see both at the same time. Some of you may see only one image until someone who sees the second image guides you to see it too. There are also people who see a third image – either they are very creative or their minds are playing tricks on them!

The mind chooses what it sees. It is not a fault of the mind, because it does not seek to validate what it sees from the outside. It depends on itself to see what it sees. If I had not mentioned the second image in the painting above, your mind might not even have entertained of the possibility.

Likewise, at work and in our daily lives, our minds often quickly home in on a particular point without allowing for other perspectives. This can lead us to hold on to beliefs in the face of all manner of evidence against it.

For example, a research study showed that after the 911 attacks, terrorist attacks by Muslims received 449% more coverage than other attacks in the US. Yet, the figures show that between 2011 and 2015, of the 89 attacks that were committed in the US, only 12.4% were carried out by Muslim perpetrators.

Sometimes in conversation, people appear to be listening to me. But are they really getting what I'm saying? Perhaps they are only listening selectively, looking out for information or keywords they want to hear and ignoring everything else. Or even if they're listening actively, perhaps they are misinterpreting my point. For example, if I were to say that John is wise, my listeners could interpret it as John being smart instead of wise because the wise men they have met in their lives have always been smart. The mind can only interpret the information it receives based on the limited knowledge it has.

A related phenomenon is telling people what they like to hear instead of what is. This could arise for many reasons, including the need for social acceptance. We know that we have a better chance of being liked by others if we say things that please them. We have also been on the receiving end, where we feel more kindly towards a person whose words touched our heart. The danger, though, is that this can lead to untruths and manipulation.

As leaders we need to pierce through this veil of seeing only what we want to see and telling only what others like to hear. This requires careful attention as well as awareness of the inner motives behind our behaviour.

Inquiry

1. Does my communication always revolve around what I want others to hear or what is?
2. How can I ensure that my team members have understood my intentions?

51

EVOLUTION VS TRANSFORMATION

There is a big difference between the birth of a mushroom and the birth of a butterfly. Mushrooms emerge in your garden overnight and they surprise you. Butterflies on the other hand go through a slow process of metamorphosis that takes several days.

When new knowledge enters our life, it naturally changes us. Some of us change like a mushroom and some of us change like a butterfly. As a leader it is important that we evolve like a butterfly rather than transform like a mushroom. The change in us should be gradual, because the human mind does not adjust to change quickly.

A person who changes overnight can face rejection from the people around him, because the sudden transformation takes away all that they knew about him. I have encountered leaders who were authoritarian the day before, and democratic the morning after. Their team members found it very difficult to accept or rationalise the sudden turnaround. They were fearful, and started asking questions like "What happened to him?"

When you bring mindfulness into your leadership, there will be changes at the level of your thoughts, feelings and actions. People around you will start noticing these changes. It is important that your change benefits not only yourself but also your team members. Your self-awareness informs you of the changes in yourself that can affect others. And you can inquire how that affects you and the well-being of others as you continue evolving as a mindful leader.

Inquiry

1. What could be the impact of Mindfulness-Informed Leadership on my leadership? How would that affect my team members?
2. How can I make it easy for people around me to adjust to my evolution?

52

RESILIENCE

I remember my father sharing with me his childhood stories of hard work and struggle. He was born at a time when Singapore was part of British Malaya. Right after he was born, the Japanese occupied Singapore. The family went through extreme hardship and eventually his father had to leave Singapore, leaving behind my father and his five siblings, as well as my grandmother. My father told me he had to wear tattered clothes to school, which embarrassed him and made him a subject of ridicule. At the age of 12 he stopped going to school so that he could start working, to support the family along with his brothers.

My mother was also born to a very large family. She was one of the top students in her class at school, but had to stop schooling at the age of 12, because her father was unable to support her education financially. It was she who coached me in my studies right up to my tenth year. Both my parents had a lot of regrets that they were not able to continue their education due to financial woes. However, that led them to want my sister and me to not be deprived of educational opportunities.

In spite of financial challenges, my early childhood was a happy one. I subconsciously learned that it is possible to be happy even if you don't own much by way of material possessions. Despite it all, my parents were successful in buying an apartment for themselves and relocating from a rural life to an urban one. With my father being the sole breadwinner, they were able to put us through school. We grew up in a lively environment filled with pets and music. My father was a musician and I remember my early home life filled with lyric books and vinyl records.

The reason I am sharing this story is to tell you that the family narratives I heard were a mix of "ascending" (rags to riches) and "descending" (riches to rags) narratives. Dr Marshall Duke of Emory University found that children who listened to only ascending narratives, or to only descending narratives, faced more difficulty handling adversity. It was the children that listened to both ascending and descending narratives that built resilience. This is so true, at least for me.

There is an important lesson here for leadership, too. Traditionally leaders tend to speak to their team members only when there are problems or challenges in their performance. Conversations don't happen when things go right. There are even some who believe that there should be zero tolerance for descending or weakness narratives. This is unhealthy because it does not contribute to wholeness. It is wholeness that creates resilience, not polarisation. Too much positivity may in fact impede the building of resilience. A balance needs to be sought. More conversations around descending narratives can help teams to continue being successful.

Inquiry

1. What are the narratives that my mind preoccupies itself with?
2. What are my popular narratives with my team members?

53

THE U-TURN

Most drivers would be very familiar with the U-turn. To make a U-turn, you have to be driving rather slowly. If you are travelling at high speed, a U-turn is impossible. It is also obviously impossible to make a U-turn if your vehicle is stationary. Furthermore, a lorry or a bus makes a U-turn differently from a car. The driver of a heavy vehicle needs to be very careful when manoeuvring it. A cargo ship has an even bigger turning radius and hence takes a bigger U-turn.

A leader is like a car, a team is like a bus, and an organisation is like a ship.

The first lesson in making a change in our lives is to slow down. Slowing down allows us to recognise the impact that the change will have on the people around us and the environment we operate in. What is positive to you may not be positive for others. Discretion is hence required when taking steps forward.

It is easier and faster to make changes as a single person. When making changes as a team, more time and effort is required. Leaders need to have patience and other-awareness in such situations. Sometimes team members can also be faster in adapting to changes than yourself, especially when it comes to technology with a younger workforce. This requires acceptance as well.

When it comes to organisations, change takes even longer. More factors have to be considered before instituting a change. That is the reason why change management strategies are recommended.

Inquiry

1. How can I effect change among my team members in a way that is palatable?
2. What kind of change is my organisation going through right now? Is it fast or slow?

54

LEARNING FROM ALL DIRECTIONS

The only thing that interferes with my learning
is my education.
— Albert Einstein

Did you hear about the 18-year-old boy who found that perforating seeds can increase yield and food production? He learned it from watching YouTube videos. Amazing, right?

Our formal education at times gives us the idea that learning takes place only when we are in a classroom, or when we are holding a book. We equate learning with education erroneously. Education is a formal system of teaching and learning which involves pedagogy. Learning is personal and reflects the assimilation of information. While both are important, it is learning that we aim for via education.

That does not mean, though, that education is useless. I compare education to a ladder that allows you to scale a wall to see what lies beyond the wall. Seeing beyond that wall is learning.

As leaders, we can learn from all directions. We can learn from our team members, bosses, workers, cleaners – anyone. I have learned so much from my conversations with cabbies, janitors, wayfarers, tourists, retail salespersons and many others. I have also learned from people who are commonly called adversaries or competitors, although I know of no such labels in the absolute sense of the word. I have even learned a lot from animals, like my pets. In an Indian mythological story, a wise man learns from 24 teachers: the earth, air, sky, fire, the sun, pigeon, python, sea, moth, elephant, ant, fish, a prostitute, an arrow-maker, a boy, the moon, honeybee, deer, bird of prey, woman, serpent, spider, caterpillar and water.

To learn, we do not need a teacher, but a learner.

Inquiry

1. What is one great leadership lesson that I learned from a supposedly insignificant person or being?
2. What makes it difficult for people to learn from someone whom they consider insignificant?

55

STAKEHOLDER MANAGEMENT

How we look at our stakeholders reflects a great deal about ourselves. A stakeholder is any person or group who is involved in or connected to your leadership goals and objectives. As leaders of teams, businesses and organisations, we have numerous stakeholders, all of whom are important.

There is a stakeholder analysis exercise where one's various stakeholders are mapped onto a matrix based on the power they wield and their level of interest in your project or business. Depending on which cell they fall into, an appropriate response is then suggested. This matrix should be used with caution – it is a good guide for general practice, but a mindful leader will go beyond this.

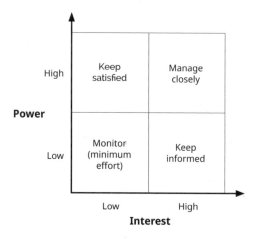

In my experience with organisations, most of us give too much attention to customers and shareholders, primarily because of the power and interest they have in our product, service or goals. We negotiate with people who have high power and interest while unconsciously manipulating people with low power and/or interest. As a result, people who have lower power and interest may be neglected.

In mindfulness we are aware that we see people as people, each performing different roles. As people we are intrinsically the same, as there is no differentiation in terms of our purpose of life. Our professional roles, however, create differences in power and interest.

People with low interest and low power are still worthy of our respect. While the matrix recommends putting in just the "minimum effort" to monitor this group of stakeholders, we must take care to treat them with wholesomeness. Mindfulness reminds us to regard all stakeholders as fellow humans first, then as the roles they play. This is how we can balance our role at work and our being.

Inquiry

1. Which stakeholders are the most important to my leadership? How much of my time and attention are invested in them?
2. Do my team members get the same attention as the important stakeholders?

56

MODELLING IT

As leaders we do not choose to become role models, but we are. We have no choice, because our decisions, beliefs and worldview sub-consciously influence our team members as they go about their work.

It is like how children inherit certain traits and behaviours from their parents. As they keep seeing and hearing what their parents do and say, they repeat the very same thing.

The same thing happens in teams. If the leader is respectful, the team is respectful. If the leader is driven and uncompromising, the team takes on these traits too. If change is desired, it must begin with the leader. We must model it first.

Here is a true story. A mother approached Mahatma Gandhi and told him that her son ate too much sugar. She asked him to advise her son to cut back on his sugar intake. Gandhi, after reflecting a bit, told her to go home and return in two weeks. She went away perplexed. Nevertheless with trust she returned in two weeks with her son. Gandhi told the boy to stop eating so much sugar as that was injurious to his health. The son promised to do so. The mother was pleased, but asked Gandhi what was the reason for the two-week wait. Gandhi responded that he had to first cut back on his own sugar intake – two weeks ago he had had an obsession for it too.

Yes, as leaders we need to model the behaviours we want to see in our team members, but more importantly, our intentions need to be wholesome. Modelling wholesomeness in thoughts, emotions and actions allows our members to be mindful as well. This is the prime purpose of Mindfulness-Informed Leadership. We inspire by walking the talk.

Inquiry

1. How can I consciously model my values for wholeness and wholesomeness?
2. What are my current behaviours (thoughts, words and actions) that resonate wholesomeness?

Epilogue: Sustenance

Congratulations on completing the 56-day journey.

You have come a long way, but the journey is not over. That's because wisdom is an evolving understanding of oneself, others and the world over time. You now have to find a way to sustain the practice of being and doing.

In the first part of the book, we looked at the case for Mindfulness-Informed Leadership, especially its relevance to the future of work. We also saw the dark and bright sides of humanity today. Leveraging on the bright side, we saw what mindfulness is and its potential in leadership and making positive change.

We then looked into the six domains of MIL – Awareness, Acceptance, Attention, Action, Attitude and Wisdom. Attitude forms the fundamental traits that we aim to develop over time. The three elements of mindfulness practices which are central to MIL are Awareness, Acceptance and Attention. Action is the domain of doing where your responses arise from your very being. And finally, all this culminates in Wisdom, which in turn impacts your attitude and action through wholeness and wholesomeness.

In the second part of the book, we took a 56-day journey to deepen our practice and appreciation of MIL. I hope this journey has been a rewarding one, especially in being – not becoming – a mindful leader.

You would have cultivated the ability to notice your thoughts, emotions and actions non-judgmentally.

Your self-awareness would have been enhanced effortlessly.

Your actions would have been wholesome and would have led towards wholeness.

Your wisdom would have evolved and you would likely be happier, with less stress.

As a result, you would have found that leading people is not for the sake of your happiness alone, but to create positive change that is wholesome for you, your team members, society and the world.

The key to sustaining the effectiveness of your leadership lies in one thing: the practice of mindfulness. Nothing else is needed. If you have not been trained in mindfulness, I would encourage you to pick it up formally through one of the 8-week programmes offered in your town. Through a formal programme, you will be able to learn these practices in a structured and systematic manner, and eventually integrate them organically into your daily living.

Thank you for picking up this book, and for your courage and willingness to try out these leadership experiments. I wish you success.

EPILOGUE: SUSTENANCE

Most of all,

May you be well

May you be happy

May you be healthy

May you be free from Suffering

This is all I wish for you.

About the Author

Kathirasan K is a Certified Mindfulness Teacher-Professional (CMT-P) and a world-renowned scholar-practitioner of the ancient Indic traditions of Meditation and Philosophy. He is the Founder CEO of the Centre for Mindfulness Singapore. Kathir is a highly sought-after consultant on the role of mindfulness in the areas of education, leadership, workplace, personal development, coaching, counselling, career development and stress management. He has trained and certified many mindfulness teachers, focusing on developing their skills to adapt the teaching of mindfulness to different cultures and settings and being ethically committed. He holds a PhD in Meditation and an MBA, and is a certified Yoga Instructor. His books include *Mindfulness in 8 Days* (2017) and *Mindfulness for the Family* (2020).